Day by Day

by Valerie Davies
Illustrated by Eira Reeves

paternoster
publishing

HUNT&
THORPE

Day by Day

by Valerie Davies
Illustrated by Eira Reeves

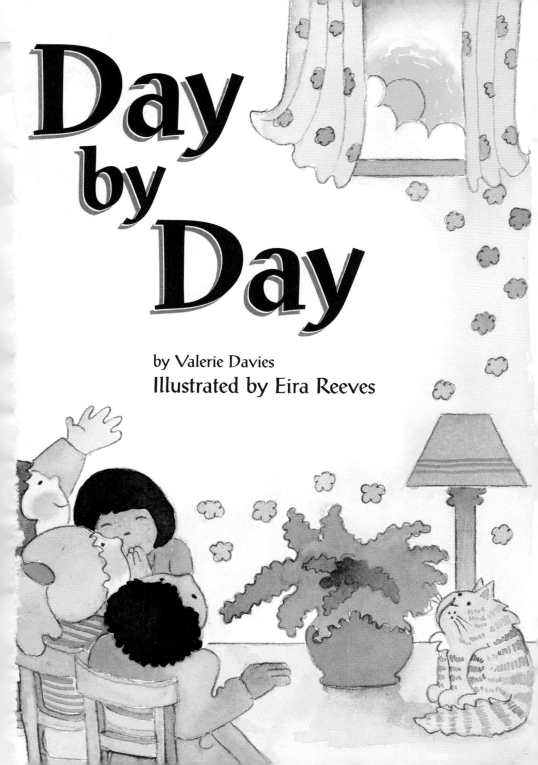

Contents

JANUARY 1

Our Father God

Bible reading: Ephesians 4 verse 6
'There is one God and Father of everything. He rules everything.
He is everywhere and in everything.'

Thought for today
Did you know that God made you? He knows you and he loves you.
God made all the people in the world - that's why he calls us his
children. He's our Father God and he looks after us.

To talk about
It's New Year's Day! Have you got a special wish or
prayer or resolve for the New Year?

A prayer to say
*Dear Father God,
thank you for
making me me.
Thank you for
loving me and
looking after me.
Amen.*

JANUARY 2

What's for ever?

Bible reading: Deuteronomy 33 verse 27
'The everlasting God is your place of safety. His arms will hold you up for ever.'

Thought for today
God has always been here and he will always be here. He lives for ever. You can't see him but he's always with you, and he always loves you.

To talk about
When we say, 'I've got butterflies in my tummy,' what do we mean? This is picture language. When we say, 'God's arms hold us up,' what do you think it means?

A prayer to say
Father God, thank you that you are always with me, and you never stop loving me. Amen.

JANUARY 3

Mighty God

Bible reading: Genesis 17 verse 1
'I am God All-Powerful. Obey me and do what is right.'

Thought for today
God is strong, and powerful and mighty. He is easily able to look after us. But he asks us to do something, too. He asks us to obey him, and trust his promises in the Bible.

To talk about:
Is there a promise in the Bible you can remember to trust or obey?

A prayer to say
Almighty, all-powerful God, help me to trust you and always do what you want me to do. Amen.

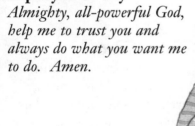

JANUARY 4

Treasure seekers

**Bible reading:
Psalm 119 verse 72**
'Your teachings are
worth more to me than
thousands of pieces of
gold and silver.'

Thought for today
Lots of people want to be rich, and to
have jewels, and thousands of pieces of gold
and silver. But better than all the treasure
in the world is the teaching of God that we
read in the Bible.

To talk about:
Do you have a favourite ornament or
piece of jewellery?

A prayer to say
*Dear Father God, help me to enjoy learning
about you. Help me to find out for myself that
your teachings are like rich treasure. Amen.*

JANUARY 5

A memory like a sieve

Bible reading: Psalm 119 verse 11
'I have taken your words to heart so I would not sin against you.'

Thought for today
'Don't touch that, it's hot,' says your mum. Soon you touch it. Why? You forgot! The man who wrote today's Bible verse kept on thinking about God's teachings. Why? He didn't want to forget and do wrong things.

To talk about
Have you ever forgotten something important?

A prayer to say
Dear Father God, help me to remember your teaching and all I learn about you. Amen.

8

JANUARY 6

The way to be wise

**Bible reading: Psalm 119
verse 130**
'Learning your words gives wisdom and understanding
for the foolish.'

Thought for today
In the Bible, a wise person is not a clever brain-box who gets top marks all
the time. Wise people are people who know how God wants them to
behave - and do it!

To talk about
Do you know any wise people?
What makes them wise?

A prayer to say
*Dear Father God, thank
you for telling us in the
Bible how to be
wise. Amen.*

JANUARY 7

A torch

Bible reading: Psalm 119 verse 105
'Your word is like a lamp for my feet and a light for my way.'

Thought for today
Think of walking along a path in the pitch-black darkness. You can't see where you're putting your feet. Ouch! You need a torch! Today's verse says that God's word in the Bible is like a torch. When we feel as though we are in the dark about what to do, it teaches us.

To talk about
When do you find a torch useful?

A prayer to say
Dear Father God, thank you for your words that are like a torch. Amen.

January 8

God's light

Bible reading:
Psalm 119 verse 105
'Your word is like a lamp for
my feet and a light for my
way.'

Thought for today
When we are in a dark room and
turn on the light we can see things
clearly. God's word in the Bible is like a
light in a dark room. It helps us to
understand what God wants us to think,
do and say.

ᏯᏬᏬᏬ
To talk about
Look back to January 2.
Can you think of another example of
picture language?

A prayer to say
*Dear Father God, help me to use your
word-torch. Help me to know how
you want me to behave.
Amen.*

This way

Bible reading: Isaiah 30 verse 21

'If you go the wrong way - to the right or to the left - you will hear a voice behind you. It will say, "This is the right way. You should go this way."'

Thought for today

Suppose you are walking to school with your mum. She meets a friend and is so busy walking and talking that she misses the turning to school. What would you say? Sometimes in our lives we might start to do wrong things. God helps us to see the right thing to do.

To talk about

What wrong things do you sometimes do?

A prayer to say

Dear Father God, when I know something is wrong, please help me to stop and do good things. Amen.

WRONG WAY

RIGHT WAY

January 10

Which way?

Bible reading: Isaiah 30 verse 21
'If you go the wrong way - to the right or to the left - you will hear a voice behind you. It will say, "This is the right way. You should go this way."'

Thought for today
Sometimes you and your family have to make decisions about what to do. Which school should you go to? Who should you invite to your party? This verse tells us that God helps us when we have to choose what to do.

To talk about
Who will you invite to your next party?

A prayer to say
Dear Father God, thank you for helping us when we have to make choices. Amen.

God is love

Bible reading: 1 John 4 verse 8

'Whoever does not love does not know God, because
God is love.'

Thought for today

What is love?
Love is patient.
Love is kind.
Love is tender.
Love is not proud, and will not think
bad things.
Love is not happy when people do wrong things.

To talk about

Today's words were written by St Paul.
What do you find hard to do in this list?

A prayer to say

*Please, heavenly Father, help me to be kind and
patient, and all the other
things that are loving.
Amen*

14

God's Son, Jesus

Bible reading: Hebrews 1 verses 2-3

'God has chosen his Son to own all things. And he made the world through the Son. The Son reflects the glory of God. He is an exact copy of God's nature.'

Thought for today

Right at the beginning of time, God the Father was not alone because Jesus was with him. They made the world together. Jesus is the same as God and he shows us God's power and love.

To talk about

Read yesterday's 'thought' and put Jesus instead of love. What do you like about Jesus?

A prayer to say

Dear Father God, thank you for sending Jesus to this world to show us what you are like. Amen.

15

JANUARY 13

God's love

Bible reading: John 3 verse 16
'For God loved the world so much that he gave his only Son. God gave his
Son so that whoever believes in him may not be lost, but have eternal life.'

Thought for today
Think of something that you love very much. It would be hard to give it
away, or even to lend it to someone else. God loved his Son Jesus very
much indeed, but God sent Jesus to this world because he loves us so much.

<hr>

To talk about
What is something you love very much?

<hr>

A prayer to say
*Dear Father God, thank you for loving all the people in the world so
much that you gave Jesus. Thank you for loving me, too. Amen.*

JANUARY 14

A tiny bird

Bible reading: Matthew 10 verse 29
'When birds are sold, two small birds cost only a penny. But not even one of the little birds can die, without your Father's knowing it.'

Thought for today
When Jesus was alive little birds were caught and sold very cheaply. Nobody thought they were important. But Jesus said that our Father God knows what happens to every tiny bird. You are far more important than a sparrow, so think how much God must care for you.

To talk about
Do you have a favourite bird?

A prayer to say
Dear Father God, thank you that you care for the little birds. Thank you that you care for me, too. Amen.

JANUARY 15

Every hair

Bible reading: Matthew 10 verses 30, 31

'God even knows how many hairs are on your head. So don't be afraid.'

Thought for today

Can you count all the hairs on your head? Jesus said that you are so precious to your heavenly Father that he even knows how many hairs you have! So he doesn't want you to be afraid or worried about anything.

To talk about
Is there something you are worried about?

A prayer to say

Heavenly Father, thank you that I am precious to you, and that you know how many hairs I have on my head. I cannot count them, they are too many! Amen.

JANUARY 16

On guard

Bible reading: Isaiah 27 verse 3

'I, the Lord, will care for that vineyard.
I will water it at the right time.
No one will hurt it. I will guard it day and night.'

Thought for today

Today's verse describes a farmer taking care of the vines in his vineyard. That is how our heavenly Father cares for us. He looks after us all the time.

To talk about

If you are given a seed, what do you have to do to make it grow?

A prayer to say

Thank you, heavenly Father, for looking after me night and day and keeping me safe.
Amen.

19

JANUARY 17

Don't be scared

Bible reading: Isaiah 41 verse 13

'I am the Lord your God. I am holding your right hand. And I tell you, "Don't be afraid. I will help you."'

Thought for today

Dark bedrooms with flapping curtains. Hairy, frisky spiders. Crashing thunder … there are lots of scary things around! Our Father God understands. He says, 'I will help you. Don't be afraid.' So tell him about it.

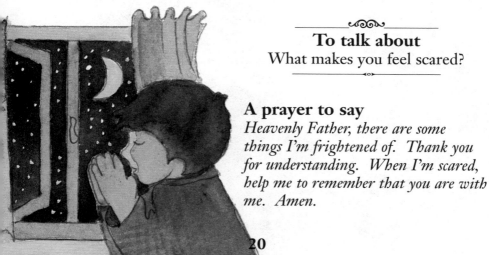

To talk about
What makes you feel scared?

A prayer to say

Heavenly Father, there are some things I'm frightened of. Thank you for understanding. When I'm scared, help me to remember that you are with me. Amen.

JANUARY 18

Help!

Bible reading: Psalm 50 verse 15
'Call to me in times of trouble. I will save you,
and you will honour me.'

Thought for today
When you fall over and cut your knee,
do you call out to Mummy for help?
She makes you feel better. As well as
calling to Mummy or Daddy, we can call out to God for
help when anything bad happens.

To talk about
Have you or has someone in your family had an accident?
What happened?

A prayer to say
*Heavenly Father, thank you
for my Mummy and Daddy
and all the other people who
help me. Thank you because
I can ask for your help, too.
Amen.*

21

January 19

Come to me

Bible reading: Matthew 11 verse 28
'Come to me, all of you who are tired and have heavy loads.
I will give you rest.'

Thought for today
When Jesus was alive, the religious leaders made up hundreds of rules.
They said that if you wanted to be good and please God, you had to keep
every one. It was hopeless! But Jesus said, 'All you need to do is trust me,
and do what I say. I will help you.'

To talk about
Do you know someone who has many problems?

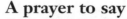

A prayer to say
*Dear Lord Jesus, thank you for coming to help
all the people who are worn out because of their
hard life and their problems and worries. Help
them to trust you. Amen.*

Strange places and new faces

Bible reading: Exodus 33 verse 14
'The Lord answered, "I myself will go with you. And I will give you victory."'

Thought for today
Kim has to go to hospital. Alex is starting a new school. They're scared! In today's Bible verse God was speaking to Moses. Moses had to take a great crowd of people across the desert to a new country full of fierce enemies. What did God say to him?

To talk about
Can you remember your first day at school or playgroup? What was it like?

A prayer to say
Dear Father God, sometimes I don't want to go to strange, new places or do hard things. Thank you that I know you will be with me. Amen.

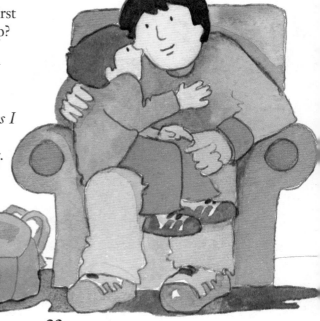

January 21

A safe place

Bible reading: Proverbs 1 verse 33
'But those who listen to me will live in safety. They will be safe, without fear of being hurt.'

Thought for today
Where is the safest place in your home? I guess it is in your mummy or daddy's arms. Our heavenly Father said that if we listen to him we shall be safe, like being in someone's arms. To listen to God means to trust and obey what he says in the Bible.

To talk about
Was there a time when you felt scared, and then your mum and dad came and you felt better?

A prayer to say
Dear heavenly Father, please help all children everywhere to feel safe in their mummy and daddy's arms.
Amen.

JANUARY 22

On guard!

Bible reading:
2 Thessalonians 3 verse 3

'But the Lord is faithful. He will give you strength and protect you...'

Thought for today

Kings, queens, presidents and other important people have guards to protect them. We are God's Very Important People and God protects us. Sometimes sad things may happen, but God doesn't let the bad things harm us. Instead he helps us to pray and trust him more than ever.

To talk about

A sad thing that has happened.
Ask God to make good come out of the sadness.

A prayer to say

Dear Father God, thank you because I don't have to be a king or queen or president before I can have a guard. You are looking after me all the time. Amen.

Countdown

Bible reading: Psalm 31 verse 15
'My life is in your hands.'

Thought for today
Every day, all day, every minute, every second, each tick of the clock, all my life, God takes care of me.

To talk about
What parts of each day do you specially enjoy?

A prayer to say
Heavenly Father, thank you for loving me all day long.
Amen.

JANUARY 24

A comforter

Bible reading:
2 Corinthians 1 verse 3
'Praise be to the God and Father of our Lord Jesus Christ. God is the
Father who is full of mercy. And he is the God of all comfort.'

Thought for today
Our Father God has given us a Comforter. 'The Holy Spirit' is God's
Comforter who is with us all the time.

To talk about
Have you got a 'comforter' - perhaps a teddy or a
doll or a comforting blanket, or your thumb?

A prayer to say
*Thank you, heavenly Father, because you know we
need comforting. Thank you for giving us the
Holy Spirit to be our Comforter. Amen.*

JANUARY 25

Worry free

Bible reading: 1 Peter 5 verse 7
'Give all your worries to him, because he cares for you.'

Thought for today
Do you sometimes get worried about things? Do you tell your mum or dad? They love you so much that they set about solving your problems. Today's verse says that God is like that. He wants us to tell him all our worries - and then we can stop worrying.

To talk about
Talk about a worry you have at the moment.

A prayer to say
Dear heavenly Father, thank you because, just like my mummy and daddy, you listen to my worries and problems, and take them away. Amen.

JANUARY 26

A brave hen

Bible reading: Psalm 91 verse 4
'He will protect you like a bird spreading its wings over its young.'

Thought for today
Have you seen a mother hen call her chicks? She flutters about after them and gathers them all under her wings to keep them safe and warm. That is how our heavenly Father feels about us. He wants to protect us.

To talk about
What would you like to say to a little chick that runs away?

A prayer to say
Dear Father God, thank you for the mother hen wanting to gather her chicks under her wings. Thank you for loving me like that.
Amen.

January 27

Counting sheep

Bible reading:
Psalm 127 verse 2
'The Lord gives sleep to those he loves.'

Thought for today

Kim can't sleep. She tosses and turns. She counts pretend sheep.
She calls her mummy and has a hot drink. It's horrid lying awake at night.
Then Kim thinks about today's verse. She tells Jesus her problems.
She sings Christian songs to herself and she drifts off into sleep.

To talk about

What do you do when you can't sleep?

A prayer to say

Dear Lord Jesus, thank you for giving us the gift of sleep. Help children who can't get to sleep to pray to you and trust you to help them. Amen.

JANUARY 28

Broken hearts

Bible reading:
Psalm 147 verse 3
'He heals the broken-hearted.
He bandages their wounds.'

Thought for today
When people feel very, very sad indeed, we say that their hearts are broken. Sometimes things get hurt and broken. We can mend many things, but only God can mend a broken heart. He sent Jesus to heal broken hearts.

To talk about
Have you ever broken anything? What happened?

A prayer to say
Heavenly Father, thank you for sending Jesus to us.
Thank you that he can heal broken hearts. Amen.

A glimpse of glory

Bible reading: Isaiah 6 verse 1

'In the year that King Uzziah died, I saw the Lord. He was sitting on a very high throne. His long robe filled the Temple.'

Thought for today

Today's verse was written by a man called Isaiah. One day God took Isaiah into heaven. He saw burning bright heavenly creatures singing praises to God, the high King of heaven. They sang, 'Holy, holy, holy, is the Lord of heaven's armies. His glory fills the whole earth.'

To talk about

When we sing hymns we are praising God. What is one of your favourite hymns?

A prayer to say

Dear Father God, I praise you, too. You are so holy, so powerful and good and loving. Amen.

A rainbow　　JANUARY 30

Bible reading: Ezekiel 1 verses 26-28

'And on the throne was a shape like a man... I saw a bright light all around him. The glow around him looked like the rainbow in the clouds on a rainy day.'

Thought for today

Ezekiel saw a rainbow in the clouds, and in the rainbow was a throne, glowing like a jewel. On the throne he saw the figure of a man shining with brilliant light, like a blazing fire. Ezekiel felt he was looking at the glory of God.

To talk about

Why do you think everybody loves rainbows?

A prayer to say

Heavenly Father, thank you for the beautiful things we see that show us how beautiful you must be. Amen.

JANUARY 31

Eureka! Now I see!

Bible reading: 2 Corinthians 4 verse 6
'God once said, "Let the light shine out of the darkness!" And this is the same God who made his light shine in our hearts. He gave us light by letting us know the glory of God that is in the face of Christ.'

Thought for today
'I don't understand!' Do you sometimes say that? Then Mummy explains, and you suddenly see what she means. When we love Jesus, and trust him, it's because God himself has helped us to see who Jesus is.

To talk about
Can you think of a time when your mum or dad helped you to understand something?

A prayer to say
Thank you, Father God, because you help me understand about Jesus. And you help my mummy and daddy as they tell me about Jesus. Amen.

When time began

Bible reading: Genesis 1 verse 3
'Then God said, 'Let there be light!'

Thought for today
Way back at the beginning of time, God made planet
Earth. It was boiling hot and black. First, God said, 'Let
there be light.' Light came, and it was good. God split
the light from the dark, and he called the light, 'day',
and the dark, 'night'. That was Day One.

To talk about
What can you do in the light that you can't do in
the pitch dark?

A prayer to say
*Dear Father God, please help blind people who
are in the pitch dark all the time.*
Amen.

FEBRUARY 2

The startling sky

Bible reading: Genesis 1 verse 8
'God named the air "sky"'

Thought for today
On Day Two of the making of planet Earth, God said, 'Let the waters above the earth separate from the waters on the earth.' God put the air all round planet Earth like a big dome, and he called the air, 'sky'.

To talk about
The sky is always changing. What sort of sky do you like best - and least?

A prayer to say
Dear Father God, thank you for air to breathe, and thank you for the enormous sky, and the clouds. Amen.

Seas and seeds

Bible reading: Genesis 1 verse 12

'The earth produced plants ... The trees made fruit with seeds in it ... God saw that all this was good.'

Thought for today

On Day Three God said, 'Let the water under the sky be gathered together so the dry land will appear.' He named the water 'sea'. Then God said, 'Let the earth have grass, and plants with seeds and trees with fruit.' And it was all good.

To talk about

Imagine a perfect picnic. Where will you be?

A prayer to say

Thank you, heavenly Father, for the sea to paddle and swim in, and for seeds that grow lovely flowers.
Amen.

FEBRUARY 4

Starry nights and sunlit days

Bible reading: Genesis 1 verse 17
'God put all these in the sky to shine on the earth.'

Thought for today
On Day Four God made the sun, the moon and the stars. Now the night was not always black and the day not always grey. Now there was a way of telling the time, and there were months and years. And now there were the seasons: spring, summer, autumn and winter.

To talk about
How can you tell that spring is coming?

A prayer to say
Thank you for the changing seasons,
for the snow and icy winds in winter,
and the hot summer sun. Amen.

FEBRUARY 5

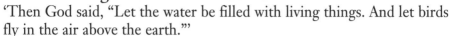

Wings and fins

Bible reading: Genesis 1 verse 20
'Then God said, "Let the water be filled with living things. And let birds fly in the air above the earth."'

Thought for today
On Day Five God made whales, and crabs, and dolphins. He made all the creatures in the seas, and lakes and streams. And he made birds of all kinds from eagles to the robin redbreast. 'Grow in numbers,' God said, 'and be happy.' And God saw that it was all good.

To talk about
Which would you rather be - a bird or a fish?

A prayer to say
Dear Father God, thank you for the fish and birds. Amen.

FEBRUARY 6

Trillions of terrestrials

Bible reading: Genesis 1 verse 31
'God looked at everything he had made, and it was very good.'

Thought for today
On Day Six God made the animals, and creepy crawly things like spiders. Last of all, he made a man and woman. God said, 'There's grain and fruit to eat. Have children, and be happy. And look after my world - I'm putting you in charge.'

To talk about
Some animals are fun to look at. What animals do you find funny?

A prayer to say
Dear Father God, thank you for all the animals, for soft rabbits and prickly hedgehogs, and for ... Help us to take good care of your world. Amen.

FEBRUARY 7

Happy days

Bible reading: Genesis 2 verse 3
'God blessed the seventh day and made it a holy day.
He made it holy because on that day he rested.'

Thought for today
On Day Seven God rested from all his work. That's why he gives us a day
each week to rest. He knows we can't work all the time. Day Seven is a
happy day, a day for relaxing from work and for praising God.

To talk about
How can we make Sundays special?

A prayer to say
Dear Father God, thank you for giving us Sundays. Amen.

41

FEBRUARY 8

The wide world

Bible reading: Psalm 104
verses 24, 10, 12, 15

'Lord, you have made many things. With your wisdom you made them all. The earth is full of your riches.'
'You make springs pour into the ravines.'
'Wild birds make nests by the water. They sing among the tree branches.'
'You give us bread that gives us strength.'

Thought for today

When God made our planet Earth, he enjoyed doing it. He said it was very good.

To talk about

If you and your family could live anywhere you wanted, where would you live?

A prayer to say

Father God, thank you for the lovely world you made for us to live in, and thank you for my home. Amen.

FEBRUARY 9

God's world

Bible reading: Psalm 24 verse 1
'The earth and everything in it belong to
the Lord. The world and all its people
belong to him.'

Thought for today
When you make something yourself it is
specially yours. You have to think about
how to do it, and work it out. Nobody
can make it like you. Because our
heavenly Father made our world, it is all
his. But he wants us to enjoy it, too.

To talk about
What do you like making?
What is one of the best things you've made?

A prayer to say
Heavenly Father, thank you for sharing your world with us.
And thank you for all the fun I have making things. Amen.

43

FEBRUARY 10

Nobody is a nobody

Bible reading: Psalm 8 verses 3 and 4

'I look at the heavens... I see the moon and stars which you created. But why is man important to you? Why do you take care of human beings?'

Thought for today

Today's verse is from an old song. Look up at the stars, it says. Look how many there are. God made them all. Does this great God care about people? Yes, he does!

To talk about

Do you know someone who everybody treats like a nobody?

A prayer to say

Dear Father God, you made all this universe. I'm so glad that you still have time and love to care for me. Amen.

FEBRUARY 11

What's in a name?

Bible reading: Matthew 1 verses 20 to 21
'The angel said ... "You will name the son Jesus. Give him that name because he will save his people from their sins."'

Thought for today
Sanjit's friends call him 'Matchstick'. Emma's nickname is 'Freckles'. What do these names tell you about Emma and Sanjit? In the Bible, names are important. Like nicknames, they were chosen because of their meaning. God chose the name of his Son. The name 'Jesus' means 'the Lord saves'.

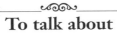
To talk about
Do any of your friends have nicknames?

A prayer to say
Dear Lord Jesus, thank you for coming to this earth to save us from wrong.
Amen.

FEBRUARY 12

Follow the leader

Bible reading: Mark 14 verses 61 and 62
"'Are you the Christ, the Son of the blessed God?'
Jesus answered, "I am.""

Thought for today
Clinton is called 'President'. Elizabeth is called
'Queen'. President and Queen are not names - they're
titles. We call Jesus 'Christ'. This is a title, too.
'Christ' means 'the great leader God has chosen to
rescue his people'.

To talk about
How can we follow Jesus?

A prayer to say
*Dear Lord Jesus, it was great news for
the world when you came to this earth.
Help me to follow you.
Amen.*

FEBRUARY 13

Name-calling

Bible reading: Acts 11 verse 26

'In Antioch the followers were called Christians for the first time.'

Thought for today

Two days ago we talked about nicknames. Today's verse is about a nickname. It's the nickname given to the first followers of Jesus - 'Christians'. It meant 'someone who belongs to Christ', Christ's boy or girl, man or woman.

To talk about

Do you know any other nicknames? Choose a good nickname for yourself?

A prayer to say

Dear Lord Jesus, when we trust you and do what you say, we belong to you. I'm glad to be a Christian. Amen.

47

FEBRUARY 14

Shepherd and sheep

Bible reading: John 10 verse 11
'Jesus said, "I am the good shepherd."'

Thought for today
Today's verse is a name Jesus gave to himself. In Bible times a shepherd chose names for his sheep. He walked on ahead, calling their names, and they followed him. He led his sheep to fields of green grass, and he kept them safe from wild animals.

To talk about
Can you think of a nursery rhyme about a lamb following someone?

A prayer to say
Dear Lord Jesus, thank you for showing us that you are the Good Shepherd. I am like your little lamb. I need never be scared.
Amen.

FEBRUARY 15

Mums and dads

Bible reading: Matthew 3 verse 17
God's voice said, 'This is my Son and I love him.
I am very pleased with him.'

Thought for today
Do you know your mum's name? Jesus' mother's name
was Mary. His stepfather was Joseph. But Jesus' real
Father is God himself. God loved Jesus very much
indeed.

To talk about
Who are the people in your family who
love you and look after you?

A prayer to say
*Dear Father God, thank you for my family, especially …
Thank you for all their love and care for me.
Amen.*

49

A fantastic family

Bible reading: 1 John 3 verse 1

'The Father has loved us so much! He loved us so much that we are called children of God. And we really are his children.'

Thought for today

Mummy, Daddy, sisters, brothers, aunts and uncles, cousins, grans and grandads. My what big families some people have! God has his family, too. Sarah, Noah, Ruth, Joseph, David, Daniel, Jonah - people who loved him in the past and all the people who love him today are part of his family.

To talk about

Can you think of someone you've read about in the Bible who you'd like to talk to in heaven?

A prayer to say

Dear Father God, thank you for all your family everywhere. Amen.

50

FEBRUARY 17

Belonging

Bible reading: John 1 verse 12

'But some people did accept him [Jesus]. They believed in him. To them he gave the right to become children of God.'

Thought for today

Today's verse tells us how to join God's family. If we believe that Jesus is God's Son who loves us, then we join God's world-wide family. Anybody at all can join.

To talk about

If someone says to you " Why should I join God's family?" What can you say?

A prayer to say

Dear Father God, thank you for loving me and wanting me to be part of your family. Amen.

FEBRUARY 18

Family problems?

Bible reading: Matthew 12 verse 50
Jesus said, 'My true brothers and sisters and mother are those who do the things that my Father in heaven wants.'

Thought for today
When Jesus was alive, he had brothers and sisters. But at first they didn't understand him or help him. That's why Jesus said the words in today's verse. His true brothers and sisters are children and grown-ups who do what God wants them to do.

To talk about
What do you do when there's a quarrel?

A prayer to say
Thank you, Lord Jesus, that when I trust you and obey you, I join your family. Amen.

FEBRUARY 19

Tastes good!

Bible reading: Ephesians 3 verse 17
Paul wrote: 'I pray that your life will be strong
in love and be built on love.'

Thought for today
Our bodies need to grow strong, so our mum
or dad give us food to eat. Our love for Jesus
needs to grow strong, too, so our Father God
gives us a special 'food'. The food that God
gives to make our love grow strong is his words
and promises in the Bible.

To talk about
What's your favourite meal?

A prayer to say
*Dear Lord Jesus, help me to think about
what you said and did so that my love and
trust can grow strong. Amen.*

FEBRUARY 20

No favourites

Bible reading: Galatians 3 verse 28
'In Christ there is no difference between Jew
and Greek ... between slaves and free men ...
between male and female. You are all the
same in Christ Jesus.'

Thought for today
In God's family every single person is as important
as every other person. Whoever you are, you are
special to God. God has no favourites.

To talk about
Are people ever mean to you or to
someone you know because of looks?

A prayer to say
*Dear Father God, help me never to be mean to children or look down on
them because of how they look. Amen.*

Stairway to heaven

Bible reading: Genesis 28 verses 16-17
'Surely the Lord is in this place ...
It is the gate of heaven.'

Thought for today
Angels are brilliant, dazzling creatures who live in
heaven. Jesus' friend, John, saw a million angels in
heaven singing praises to God. Another man, Jacob,
saw a staircase from earth to heaven, with angels
going up and down.

To talk about
Jacob was in a dark, lonely place, but who was with him?

A prayer to say
(This is part of the angels' song.)
All praise and honour and glory
and power to the One
who sits on the
throne. Amen.

FEBRUARY 22

Danger at sea

Bible reading: Acts 27:23
'Last night an angel from God came to me. This is the God I worship.'

Thought for today
The word 'angel' means 'messenger'. St Paul, a follower of Jesus, was once in a terrible storm. The ship was breaking up and the sailors were in a panic. In the night an angel came with a message from God: 'Don't be afraid. God will save all your lives.'

To talk about
Do you know the name of the angel messenger who came to Mary?

A prayer to say
Heavenly Father, thank you for sending the angel with the message to Paul. Amen.

FEBRUARY 23

An invisible army

Bible reading: 2 Kings 6 verse 17
'He saw that the mountain was full of horses and chariots of fire.'

Thought for today
Mostly angels are invisible, but sometimes God lets us see them. Once an enemy army attacked a city. A servant boy was terrified, but his master Elisha prayed, 'Lord, open my servant's eyes.' Then the boy saw God's angel army, horses and chariots of fire, all over the mountains around the enemy.

To talk about
The rest of the story is about a trick Elisha
played on the enemy.
Have you ever played a trick on
someone (perhaps on April Fool's Day)?

A prayer to say
Dear Father God, I can't see you, or your angels, but thank you because I know you are with me. Amen.

FEBRUARY 24

A wise donkey

Bible reading: Numbers 22 verse 23
'The donkey saw the angel of the Lord standing in the road. The angel had a sword in his hand.'

Thought for today
A man called Balaam was riding along a country track when an invisible angel blocked his path. The donkey saw the angel and swerved to the side. Balaam hit his donkey and the angel disappeared. Three times this happened. Then Balaam at last saw the angel. The angel said that the donkey had saved Balaam's life.

To talk about
Have you ever found that animals see or smell things we are not aware of?

A prayer to say
Dear Lord Jesus, help me always to be kind to my pets. Amen.

In disguise

Bible reading: Hebrews 13 verses 2 and 3
'Welcome strangers into your homes. Some people have done this and have welcomed angels without knowing it.'

Thought for today
Sometimes angels look like lightning and wear shining white clothes. Sometimes they are disguised as ordinary people. Abraham was once sitting outside his tent when he saw three men coming near. He thought they were desert travellers, and gave them a meal. But they were angels with a message from God.

To talk about
Do you know a child who is lonely who you could invite to play?

A prayer to say
Dear Father God, help me to be welcoming and friendly to other children, especially new children.
Amen.

FEBRUARY 26

The lions' den

Bible reading: Daniel 6 verse 23

'They lifted Daniel out and did not find any injury on him. This was because Daniel had trusted in his God.'

Thought for today

Sometimes angels rescue people from danger. Daniel would not worship an idol. So he was thrown into a den of roaring, ravenous lions. But God sent an angel into the lions' den, who closed the lions' mouths. Daniel didn't have a single scratch.

To talk about

Why did God keep Daniel safe?

A prayer to say

Dear Father God, thank you for sending the angel to keep Daniel safe. Amen.

FEBRUARY 27

Escape from prison

Bible reading: Acts 12 verse 7
'Suddenly, an angel of the Lord stood there. A light shined in the room.'

Thought for today
Peter had been thrown into prison for preaching about Jesus. He was chained between two guards. In the night an angel woke Peter up. 'Hurry, follow me.' The chains fell off and Peter followed the angel. The prison doors opened by themselves. Peter thought he was dreaming till he found himself safe in the street.

To talk about
Some people are in prison today just because they are Christians. How can we help them?

A prayer to say
Dear Jesus, please send your angels to comfort people who are in prison for preaching about you. Amen.

FEBRUARY 28

A desert meal

Bible reading: 1 Kings 19 verse 5
'Suddenly, an angel came to him and touched him. The angel said, "Get up and eat."'

Thought for today
Sometimes God sends an angel on an errand to cheer someone up. Evil Queen Jezebel vowed to kill Elijah and so he ran for his life. All alone in the desert, exhausted, hungry and very, very sad, he fell asleep. An angel woke Elijah, and he saw a glowing fire, with hot bread baking on it.

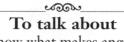

To talk about
Do you know what makes angels happy?
The answer is Luke 15 verse 10.

A prayer to say
Dear Father God, when people are tired and sad, help me to be kind to them. Amen.

FEBRUARY 29

God's secret agents

Bible reading: Psalm 34 verse 7
'The Lord saves those who fear him.
His angel camps around them.'

Thought for today
Angels are still at work today.
They still bring messages from
God, protect us from danger, and
help us when we are sad or afraid.
It is God who sends the angels, because he loves us so much.

To talk about
What have you found out about angels?

A prayer to say
*Dear Father God, thank you for angels,
your secret agents in the world.
Amen.*

MARCH 1

Hurrah for holidays

Bible reading Luke 2 verse 41
'Every year Jesus' parents went to
Jerusalem for the Passover Feast.'

Thought for today
It was holiday time for twelve-year-old Jesus, and he was very
excited. For the first time in his life he was going to Jerusalem to
visit the Temple (a bit like a big, beautiful church). The family set
off with all their friends and after a long walk they arrived.

To talk about
When it's holiday time, where is
your favourite place to go?

A prayer to say
*Thank you, Father
God, for holidays and
for special days when
we can be with our
families. Amen.*

MARCH 2

Lost!

Bible reading Luke 2 verses 44-45
'Joseph and Mary travelled for a whole day.
They thought that Jesus was with them in the group.
Then they began to look for him … they did not find him.'

Thought for today
Mary and Joseph were on their way back home from Jerusalem. They thought Jesus was with their friends. But when evening came, they couldn't see him anywhere. They rushed back to Jerusalem to find him.

To talk about
Has something frightening or exciting ever happened on a trip away from home?
What did your mum or dad do?

A prayer to say
Dear Father God, thank you for keeping me safe. Amen.

MARCH 3

Found!

Bible reading Luke 2 verses 46-47

'Jesus was sitting in the Temple with the religious teachers, listening to them and asking them questions. All who heard him were amazed at his understanding and wise answers.'

Thought for today

At last Mary and Joseph found Jesus. He was in the Temple courtyard. The religious leaders used to hold open-air discussions about the teaching of the Bible, and Jesus was listening and joining in.

To talk about

What is your favourite Bible story?

A prayer to say

Dear heavenly Father, thank you that we can learn about you even when we are very young. Amen.

Problems

Bible reading Luke 2 verses 48-49

'When Jesus' parents saw him, they were amazed. His mother said to him, "Son, why did you do this to us? Your father and I were very worried about you."... Jesus asked, "Why did you have to look for me?"'

Thought for today

Jesus had thought his parents would know he was in the Temple. They loved him but they didn't understand.

To talk about

Have you ever been in trouble when it wasn't your fault? Have you ever felt sad and thought, 'Why didn't she understand?'

A prayer to say

Dear Lord Jesus, thank you because you always understand how I feel. And thank you for my parents who love me. Amen.

March 5

Why?

Bible reading Luke 2 verse 49
'Jesus asked, "Why did you have to look for me? You should have known that I must be where my Father's work is!"'

Thought for today
Very gently Jesus said to Joseph and Mary, "Why did you get upset? Don't you understand I had to be in my Father's house?" Jesus loved his heavenly Father. He wanted to learn about him and obey him.

To talk about
Where can we learn about Jesus?

A prayer to say
Dear Father God, thank you that I am never too young to do what you want me to do. Amen.

Learning days

Bible reading Luke 2 verse 51
'Jesus went with them to Nazareth and obeyed them.'

Thought for today
The holiday was over, and Jesus went back home with Mary and Joseph. Joseph was a carpenter, and he taught Jesus to be a carpenter, too. Jesus did everything that Mary and Joseph told him to do and he grew up wise and strong.

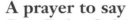

To talk about
What are some of the things you like to do and learn about?

A prayer to say
Dear Father God, help me to be loving and obedient, like Jesus. Thank you for all the things there are to learn about. Amen.

MARCH 7

12 special friends

Bible reading Mark 3 verses 14-19
'Jesus chose 12 men and called them
apostles. He wanted these 12 to be with him,
and he wanted to send them to other places
to preach.'

Thought for today
When Jesus was grown up, he started to teach
everyone about God. And he chose twelve special friends
to help him. These are their names: Peter, Matthew,
James, Thomas, John, James, Andrew, Thaddaeus, Philip, Simon,
Bartholomew, and Judas.

To talk about
Do you sometimes help your teacher at school?
What do you like to do?

A prayer to say
*Dear Lord Jesus, when I have jobs to
do, I know that you help me to do
them. Thank you, Jesus. Amen.*

The happy people

Bible reading Matthew 5 verse 1

'Jesus saw the crowds who were there. He went up on a hill and sat down. His followers came to him. Jesus taught the people.'

Thought for today

One day Jesus sat down on the hillside and told his friends how to be happy. The happy people, he said, are poor people who are peaceful, gentle and kind. They depend on God to help them in their difficulties and God makes them happy.

To talk about

Is there something you find hard to do?

A prayer to say

Dear Lord Jesus, thank you for coming to teach us about our heavenly Father. Amen.

Not now, dear!

Bible reading Mark 10 verses 13-14

'Some people brought their little children to Jesus ... But his followers told the people to stop bringing their children to him. When Jesus saw this ... he said to them , "Let the little children come to me. Don't stop them."

Thought for today

Do you have a lovely grandad or grandma, or an aunt or uncle who you go to? Someone who always has time for you, and hugs you and listens to you. Jesus was like that. He was never too busy.

To talk about

Who are your favourite grown-ups?

A prayer to say

Dear Lord Jesus, thank you for grown-ups who show us your love. Amen.

MARCH 10

A happy meal

Bible reading Matthew 8 verse 15
'Jesus touched her hand, and the fever left her.'

Thought for today
Jesus' friend, Peter, asked Jesus to come to his house for dinner. Peter's mother-in-law was ill in bed but Jesus touched her hand, and she was well again. She got up straight away and cooked dinner for them all.

To talk about
Do you know someone who is ill who you can pray for?

A prayer to say
Dear Lord Jesus, thank you for making Peter's wife's mother better again. Please will you make ... better, too. Amen.

MARCH 11

Feeling ill

Bible reading Luke 8 verse 54

'Jesus took her by the hand, and called to her, "My child, stand up!"'

Thought for today

One day a man called Jairus was extremely sad because his daughter was very ill. He went rushing into town and found Jesus. Then a man ran up. 'Your daughter has died,' he said. But Jesus said, 'Don't be afraid. Believe in me.' And Jesus brought the girl back to life again.

To talk about

When you are ill, what helps you to feel better?

A prayer to say

Dear Jesus, thank you for making the little girl well. Thank you for loving me and helping me when I feel ill. Amen.

Robbers

Bible reading Luke 10 verse 30
'Jesus said, "A man was going down the road from Jerusalem to Jericho..."'

Thought for today
Suddenly robbers pounced on that traveller, and beat him up. A priest came by and a priest's helper, but they didn't stop. Then an enemy came up. The enemy bandaged the man's wounds and took him to an inn. Jesus said, 'You must help anyone who needs your help.'

To talk about
Who are the lonely children in your class?
Who are the bullies?
Are there any ways of helping them?

A prayer to say
Dear Lord Jesus, please help me to help people, even if they don't like me. Amen.

The lost sheep

Bible reading Luke 15 verse 3

'Then Jesus told them this story: "Suppose one of you has 100 sheep, but he loses one of them ..."'

Thought for today

The shepherd in Jesus' story left his ninety-nine sheep safe in the fold and hunted everywhere for that lost sheep. At last he found it! He carried it home, and was so happy that he called out to all his friends, 'Great news! I've found my lost sheep.'

To talk about

Have you ever lost a toy, or your pet? How did you feel? What did you do?

A prayer to say

Dear Lord Jesus, thank you that the lost sheep was found. Thank you for loving me. Amen.

MARCH 14

A tiny seed

Bible reading Matthew 13 verse 31
'Jesus told another story: "The kingdom of heaven is like a mustard seed. A man plants the seed in his field ..."

Thought for today
A mustard seed is tiny. But when you plant it, it grows till it is one of the biggest of all the plants. When people obey Jesus they join God's kingdom. It started off very small, but today millions of people all over the world belong to God's kingdom.

To talk about
How do you join God's kingdom?

A prayer to say
Dear Father God, may your kingdom come, may your will be obeyed, on earth, as it is in heaven. Amen.

A storm

Bible reading Mark 4 verses 39-40

'Jesus said, "Quiet! Be still!"... He said to the disciples, "Why are you afraid? Do you still have no faith?"'

Thought for today

Jesus said to his friends, 'Let's sail across the lake.' Then he fell fast asleep in the boat ... A storm blew up. The wind howled. Giant waves broke against the boat. Jesus' friends woke Jesus up and shouted, "We're drowning. Don't you care?" Jesus stood up and stopped the storm.

To talk about

What makes you feel frightened? What do you do?

A prayer to say

Dear Lord Jesus, thank you for saving your friends in the storm. Help me to trust you when I'm scared. Amen.

MARCH 16

An amazing picnic

Bible reading Matthew 14 verse 17
'But we have only five loaves of bread and two fish.'

Thought for today
Jesus had been teaching all day. There was a great crowd of people, all tired and hungry. 'Send the people home,' said Jesus' friends. 'First, give them something to eat,' said Jesus. 'But we only have five loaves and two fish,' they said. With that food Jesus fed all the people.

A prayer to say
Dear Lord Jesus, thank you for feeding all those people. Thank you for my meals, too. Amen.

MARCH 17

Knock! Knock! Who's there?

Bible reading Luke 11 verse 9
'I tell you, continue to ask, and God will give to you.'

Thought for today
Jesus told this story. Pretend it's late at night. Without telling you, friends come. They're hungry but you've run out of food. Your dad goes next door and rings the bell. 'Can you lend us some food?' he calls out. 'At this time of night? You must be joking!' shouts your neighbour out of his bedroom window. In the end your neighbour gives your dad some food to make him go away.

To talk about
What good things can you ask God for?

A prayer to say
Thank you, Jesus, because you are not like that neighbour. You want us to keep on asking for your help. You never get tired of our prayers. Amen.

MARCH 18

Three cheers for Jesus

Bible reading Mark 11 verse 9
'God bless the One who comes in the name of the Lord.'

Thought for today
Two miles outside Jerusalem, Jesus told his friends to bring him a donkey. He was going to ride into Jerusalem. His friends cut down palm branches and spread them on the road. The crowds of visitors cheered. But the city leaders were jealous. 'We must get rid of him,' they said.

To talk about
Why do you think this Sunday is always Palm Sunday?

A prayer to say
Dear Lord Jesus, I would have joined in the procession and cheered you. I want to say, 'Praise Jesus, our King.' Amen.

MARCH 19

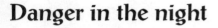

Danger in the night

Bible reading Matthew 27 verse 1
'All the leading priests and older leaders of the people decided to kill Jesus.'

Thought for today
It was Thursday night, four days after Jesus rode into Jerusalem on a donkey.
Jesus was on the hillside, praying. Suddenly there was a noise, tramping feet, bright lights, soldiers. Jesus' enemies had come. They arrested him, and took him away.

To talk about
Why didn't Jesus run away?

A prayer to say
Dear Lord Jesus, thank you for loving us so much that you came to this earth to die for us. Amen.

MARCH 20

At Skull Hill

Bible reading Luke 23 verse 33
'Jesus and the two criminals were taken to a place called the Skull. There the soldiers nailed Jesus to his cross.'

Thought for today
Jesus' enemies put him on trial. They told lies about him and sentenced him to be killed. Outside the city walls, Jesus died on a cross. He died so that we can be friends with God. Jesus' enemies thought that was the end of Jesus - they were in for a big surprise.

To talk about
Why do you think this day is called 'Good Friday' and not 'Bad Friday'?

A prayer to say
Dear Lord Jesus, thank you for your wonderful love. Thank you for dying for us. Amen.

Soldiers shiver

Bible reading
Matthew 27 verse 60
'He put Jesus' body in a new tomb that he had cut in a wall of rock.'

Thought for today
Jesus' friends wrapped his body in cloths, and put it in a cave. They rolled a big stone in front of the opening. Roman soldiers stood on guard outside the tomb. Very early Sunday morning, there was an earthquake. An angel as bright as lightning, rolled the stone away. The soldiers were petrified!

To talk about
Do you know what happened next?

A prayer to say
Dear Father God, thank you for the angel, and the rolled-away stone. Thank you for bringing Jesus back to life. Amen.

MARCH 22

A stupendous surprise

Bible reading Matthew 28 verses 5-6
'The angel said to the women, "Don't be afraid. I know that you are looking for Jesus … But he is not here. He has risen …"'

Thought for today
Early on Sunday morning some women friends of Jesus had a stupendous surprise. Very sadly they had gone to see the tomb and they were amazed to see an angel who told them that Jesus was alive! The women raced back into Jerusalem to tell Jesus' friends.

To talk about
What is the best surprise you've ever had?

A prayer to say
Dear Lord Jesus, we are so happy. You are alive! When I have the chance, help me to tell my friends. Amen.

MARCH 23

A close encounter of an exciting kind

Bible reading Luke 24 verses 32
'They said to each other … "It was exciting when he explained the true meaning of the Scriptures."'

Thought for today
'He can't be alive. The women must be dreaming.' That's what the two friends said as they walked home from Jerusalem on Easter Sunday evening. A stranger joined them. 'It's late, stay with us,' they said. At supper, when the stranger said grace, they recognised him. It was Jesus! Then Jesus disappeared.

To talk about
What do you think his two friends did next?

A prayer to say
Dear Jesus, thank you for walking with your friends on the road home. We're so glad you are alive. Amen.

MARCH 24

Ghosts don't eat

Bible reading Luke 24 verse 36
'Jesus said to them, "Peace be with you."'

Thought for today
Remember the two friends we read about yesterday? They rushed to Jerusalem to an upstairs room, where all Jesus' friends were together. 'We've seen Jesus!' they said. Suddenly Jesus was there in the room. Some people were terrified because they thought he must be a ghost. Jesus said, 'Have you any food?' They all stared while Jesus ate some fish. Ghosts don't eat!

To talk about
When you have good news to talk about, who do you tell?

A prayer to say
Dear Jesus, thank you because I know you are really alive - not a dream or a ghost. Amen.

87

MARCH 25

A test for Thomas

Bible reading John 20 verse 29
'Those who believe without seeing me will be truly happy.'

Thought for today
'Jesus is alive,' Jesus' friends said to Thomas. 'Impossible!' said Thomas. 'I'll only believe if I see him and touch him for myself.' A week later, Jesus came again to the upstairs room, and this time Thomas was there, too. 'Touch me for yourself,' Jesus said to Thomas. 'Stop doubting and believe.'

To talk about
Do you know anybody like Thomas?
What can you say to someone who doesn't believe in Jesus?

A prayer to say
Dear Lord Jesus, when Thomas did not believe in you, you didn't shout at him. You helped him to believe. Please help ... to trust you. Amen.

MARCH 26

Saying goodbye

Bible reading Luke 24 verse 48

'Jesus said, "You must tell people to change their hearts and lives. You must start at Jerusalem and preach these things in my name to all nations."'

Thought for today

Before Jesus left to go back home to his Father in heaven, he said goodbye to his friends. And he gave them a job to do. He told them to tell everybody about him.

To talk about

Who do you know who has the job of telling people about Jesus?

A prayer to say

Dear Father God, please help all missionaries. And please help ... who teaches us about your love for us. Amen.

MARCH 27

Going home

Bible reading Acts 1 verse 9
'As they were watching, he was lifted up.
A cloud hid him from their sight.'

Thought for today
Jesus had finished the work that he came to do. Now his
friends would carry on his work. In the hills outside Jerusalem
Jesus prayed for his friends. Then he was lifted up, and a cloud hid him.
Jesus had gone home to his Father in heaven.

To talk about
When you have been away on holiday,
what do you like best about coming home?

A prayer to say
*Dear Lord Jesus, thank you for my home. Please help children without a
proper home. Please help all people who work with refugees. Amen.*

MARCH 28

Good heavens!

Bible reading John 14 verse 2
Jesus said, 'There are many rooms in my Father's house ... I am going there to prepare a place for you.'

Thought for today
Jesus said today's words to his friends on the night before he died. Now he is a great King in his Father's house - in heaven - where he is praying for us. Everyone who trusts him will go to be with him in heaven, and he is waiting to welcome us.

To talk about
Some words have two meanings. Do you know the two different meanings for post, ball, heaven?

A prayer to say
Dear Lord Jesus, thank you for telling us that you are going to prepare a home for us in heaven. Amen.

thank you Jesus

thank you for heaven

MARCH 29

All change

Bible reading Revelation 21 verse 1
'Then I saw a new heaven and a new earth.'

Thought for today
There are a lot of nasty and wrong things in our world.
But one day God is going to make a new world for his people.

To talk about
What would you like to change or get rid of in this world?

A prayer to say
Dear Father God, thank you that everyone who loves you will see your new world. Amen.

March 30

Songs for sighs

Bible reading Revelation 21 verse 4
'He will wipe away every tear from their eyes. There will be no more death, sadness, crying, or pain. All the old ways are gone.'

Thought for today
A flower grows from a tiny brown seed. A butterfly from a cocoon that has once been a crawly caterpillar. Who would have guessed?
We don't know what God's new world will look like. But we do know that it will be beautiful. There will be music and singing and no more sadness.

To talk about
What beautiful things will you like to have in God's new world?

A prayer to say
Dear Father God, thank you that our new home will be happy and full of love and no one will be sad. Amen.

MARCH 31

Tigers and lions and bears

Bible reading Isaiah 11 verse 6

'Then wolves will live in peace with lambs. And leopards will lie down to rest with goats. Calves, lions and young bulls will eat together. And a little child will lead them.'

Thought for today

God's new world will be a wonderful place. There will be no more fighting. All the animals will live peacefully together. Lions will eat; grass snakes won't be poisonous. Children will play safely with the animals. And everybody will know and love God.

A prayer to say

Thank you, heavenly Father, because the animals will not kill in your new world. Amen.

To talk about

What is your favourite animal?

APRIL 1

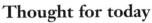

Dad alert

Bible reading: Luke 11 verse 2

Jesus said … 'When you pray, say: Father, we pray that your name will always be kept holy. We pray that your kingdom will come.'

Thought for today

Jesus' friends asked him to teach them how to pray. So Jesus taught them a prayer. The first word in the prayer is: 'Father'. How wonderful that we have a heavenly Father! He's the Father all our dads ought to be like.

To talk about

What do you think it's important for a dad to be like or to do?

A prayer to say

Dear Father God, please help everybody to do what you want, beginning with me. Amen.

APRIL 2

Everyday talk

Bible reading: Luke 11 verse 3
'Give us the food we need for each day.'

Thought for today
'Food' means the food we eat - and everything else we need to grow strong and well in our bodies, and minds and feelings and spirits (the part of us that loves God). Our Father God knows what's best for us, but he still wants us to talk to him about everything we need.

To talk about
What are Alex and Sarah doing in today's picture?

A prayer to say
Thank you, heavenly Father, for all that you give me each day. Please help children who have very little. Amen.

APRIL 3

I'm sorry

Bible reading: Luke 11 verse 4
'Forgive us the sins we have done.'

Thought for today
Sometimes we're naughty and we do things that are not kind. In the Bible this is called 'sin'. It makes everybody sad. If we say we're sorry to God, he forgives us, and he helps us to say sorry to the people we've hurt, and to be loving instead.

To talk about
Why is Sarah crying?

A prayer to say
Dear Father God, I'm sorry for …
Please forgive me. Amen.

APRIL 4

Forever friends

Bible reading: Luke 11 verse 4
'Forgive us the sins we have done, because we forgive every person who has done wrong to us.'

Thought for today
If someone is unkind to us, we feel sad. Perhaps we feel angry and want to pay them back. Can you remember when you upset someone? Afterwards you felt sorry. The person who upset you may feel sorry, too.

To talk about
If someone says to you, " I'm sorry," what does Jesus say you should do? (Look back at today's verse.)

A prayer to say
Dear Father God, please help me to be loving when someone is sorry. Amen.

APRIL 5

On the victory side

Bible reading: Luke 11 verse 4
'And do not cause us to be tested.'

Thought for today
Sometimes we say, 'Do not lead us into temptation.'
Temptation has more than one meaning. Here,
temptation or 'tested' means any very bad thing or
person, anything that stops us trusting God. Jesus is
telling us to ask God to keep us safe from being harmed
- and he does!

To talk about
Today's picture is about a different kind of
temptation. What's Alex thinking?

A prayer to say
Dear Father God, thank you for loving me.
Please keep me safe from all wrong things. Amen.

APRIL 6

A do and a don't

Bible reading: Philippians 4 verse 6
'Do not worry about anything. But pray and ask God for everything you need.'

Thought for today
Sometimes people may say that God is so big, and clever, and important and busy that he's got no time for you and me. But listen to today's verse again. What are we to pray about? What are we told NOT to do?

To talk about
Is there something you specially need at the moment?

A prayer to say
Thank you, Father God, that you want me to talk to you and to tell you about the sad things, and happy things each day. Amen.

Thanks a million

Bible reading: Philippians 4 verse 6

'Do not worry about anything. But pray and ask God for everything you need. And when you pray, always give thanks.'

Thought for today

Yesterday we said we can talk to God about everything we need. But prayer is not only asking for things. It's also thanking God for all that he's given us. Listen to today's verse again. When does it say we are to give thanks?

To talk about

Is there something happy you can thank God for?

A prayer to say

Thank you God for… And thanks for always listening to me. Amen.

APRIL 8

More than one answer

Bible reading: Isaiah 58 verse 9
'Then you will call to the Lord, and the Lord will answer you.'

Thought for today
On the bush were big, juicy, black berries. It was such a hot day and Alex was so thirsty. 'Please can I have a berry,' he begged. 'No,' his mum said. 'They're poisonous.'

When we ask God for something he always answers, but sometimes he might say 'no' or 'wait'.

To talk about
When does God say "No" to us?

A prayer to say
Dear Father God, thank you because you always know what's best for me. Amen.

APRIL 9

The maker's book

Bible reading:
2 Timothy 3 verse 16
'All Scripture is given by God and is useful for teaching and for showing people what is wrong in their lives.'

Thought for today
Suppose your mum has a new washing machine. The plumber has fixed it up. Now he's gone. Oh dear! Your mum's got a bad memory. She's forgotten how to work it. It's all right. She's found the washing-machine-maker's instruction book. Today's verse says that the Bible is God's instruction book.

To talk about
Who's good at understanding machines in your family? What happens when something breaks?

A prayer to say
Dear Father God, you made us, so you know how it's best for us to live. Thank you for giving us a book to tell us. Amen.

Tuned in

Bible reading: 1 Samuel 3 verse 10
'The Lord said ... "Samuel, Samuel!" Samuel said, "Speak, Lord, I am your servant, and I am listening."'

Thought for today
When Samuel was a boy, he didn't have a Bible like ours. When God wanted to speak to Samuel, he had to call out loud. Usually today we read God's messages in our Bibles. But however God speaks to us, he wants us to pay attention - just like Samuel.

To talk about
How can we tell when God is saying something to us?

A prayer to say
Dear Father God, help me to pay attention when I listen to stories about you. Help me to know if you are giving me a thought specially from you. Amen.

APRIL 11

Double-Dutch?

Bible reading: Luke 8 verse 9
'Jesus' followers asked him, "What does this story mean?"'

Thought for today
Look back to April 9th. Your mum's now reading the washing machine maker's book. But she can't understand it! What now? She phones the shop, and they tell her how to start the machine. We have God's book, the Bible, but often it's hard to understand. If we ask Jesus, he will help us.

To talk about
Who are the people you ask about different problems?

A prayer to say
Dear Lord Jesus, please help me to understand your teaching and stories in the Bible. Amen.

APRIL 12

'I'll show you.'

Bible reading: Matthew 9 verse 9
'When Jesus was leaving, he saw a man named Matthew ... Jesus said to him, "Follow me."'

Thought for today
Did you go to school today? And did the teacher show you how to do things? Well our heavenly Father sent Jesus into the world to show us how he wants us to live.

To talk about
What do you like about Jesus?

A prayer to say
Dear Father God, thank you for my school and my teacher. And thank you for sending Jesus to show me how you want me to live. Amen.

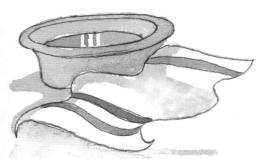

APRIL 13

Bossy-boots and servants

Bible reading: John 13 verses 14 and 15
'Jesus said, "I, your Lord and Teacher, have washed your feet …"I did this as an example for you. So you should do as I have done."'

Thought for today
Is it right to pray? What did Jesus do? Is it wrong to be mean and bossy? What did Jesus say? Jesus is our example. Today's passage means that we are not to be big-headed, but we are to look after each other.

To talk about
Can you think of something you can do that copies what Jesus would do?

A prayer to say
Thank you, heavenly Father, that you sent Jesus to be our example.
Amen.

APRIL 14

Seeing is believing

Bible reading: Romans 1 verse 20

'There are things about God that people cannot see his eternal power ... but since the beginning of the world those things have been easy to understand. They are made clear by what God has made.'

Thought for today

Have you got a picture book without any words? You can learn a lot by looking at pictures. Today's verse is from a letter written by a man called Paul. Paul says you can learn a lot about God just by looking at the world he's made.

To talk about

What do you think we can learn about God as we look at the world he's made

A prayer to say

Dear Father God, thank you for the wonderful world you have made which teaches us about you. Amen.

APRIL 15

Flower power

Bible reading: Matthew 6 verse 29
Jesus said, 'I tell you that even Solomon with his riches was not dressed as beautifully as one of these flowers.'

Thought for today
Jesus said that we can learn about God by looking at wild flowers. Our Father God dresses flowers in glorious, kingly robes. We are more important than flowers. So our mums and dads must not worry about money. God will look after us if we will trust him and obey him.

To talk about
What's your favourite flower? Why do you like it?

A prayer to say
Thank you for the beautiful flowers. Amen.

Sun and rain

Bible reading: Matthew 5 verse 45

Jesus said, 'Your Father causes the sun to rise on good people and on bad people. Your Father sends rain to those who do good and to those who do wrong.'

Thought for today

We can learn about God by looking at the sun and rain. Jesus said that God is kind even to bad people. He gives all people sunshine and rain for their crops. When people are nasty to us, we must not be mean back to them.

To talk about

Do you know someone who's mean to you or to someone else?

A prayer to say

Dear Father God, thank you because you are loving to all people. Amen.

APRIL 17

A silly builder

Bible reading: Matthew 7 verse 24

Jesus said, 'Everyone who hears these things I
say and obeys them is like a wise man. The
wise man built his house on a rock.'

Thought for today

That wise man had to dig deep to find the
firm rock. But in the storm his house was
safe. The stupid man built his house on sand.
And what happened in the storm? The
rainwater washed the sand away and the
house fell with a crash!

──────── ∽◦∾ ────────

To talk about

What's the best thing you've ever built? Would
you rather build with lego, or bricks or clay or
sand or - what?

────────────────────

A prayer to say

*Dear Father God, help me to be like the
wise man, and do things you tell me to do.
Amen.*

111

APRIL 18

Like Jesus

Bible reading: John 13 verse 34
'Jesus said … "I give you a new command: love each other. You must love each other as I have loved you."'

Thought for today
What does Jesus tell us to do in today's verse? To love people as Jesus loves us means to do all we can to help people love God. To love people means to help them be the best people they can be for God.

To talk about
Who are some of the people you love?

A prayer to say
Dear Father God, bless my mummy and daddy, because I love them. Amen.

APRIL 19

Trash!

Bible reading: Ephesians 4 verse 25

'So you must stop telling lies. Tell each other the truth ....'

Thought for today

Can you imagine Jesus telling a lie?
Children and grown-ups tell lies to make things easy for themselves. You don't tell lies to people you love and respect. Lies are trash! Throw them in the bin!

To talk about
When do children tell lies?

A prayer to say
Dear Father God, please help me not to tell lies. Amen.

Loving is for ever

**Bible reading:
Ephesians 4 verse 32**
'Be kind and loving to each other.'

Thought for today
Sometimes people cannot do things we can do. Perhaps they are sick or disabled. That is when we can be helpful and care for them. That is when we can make them happy, and God too.

To talk about
Is there someone in your family or street who's weak and needs help?

A prayer to say
Heavenly Father, please bless the people who are not able to do the things I can do. Help me to be kind and loving. Amen.

APRIL 21

A grin or a groan?

**Bible reading:
2 Corinthians 9
verse 7**
'God loves the person
who gives happily.'

Thought for today

Paul wrote today's words to some rich Christians when he was asking them
to give money to poor Christians. But he said that they mustn't be grumpy
when they gave the money. They mustn't grumble and groan. Why not?
What does today's verse say?

To talk about

There's lots of ways of giving,
even when we have no money.
Can you think of any?

A prayer to say

*Dear Father God, when I have the chance to
give anything, help me to be glad. Amen.*

APRIL 22

Miriam on guard duty

**Bible reading:
Exodus 2 verse 4**
'[Miriam] the baby's sister
stood a short distance
away ...'

Thought for today
'Kill all the baby boys,'
said the king. But Miriam
and her mother hid

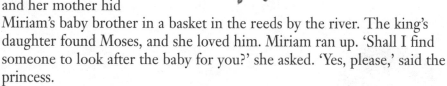

Miriam's baby brother in a basket in the reeds by the river. The king's
daughter found Moses, and she loved him. Miriam ran up. 'Shall I find
someone to look after the baby for you?' she asked. 'Yes, please,' said the
princess.

To talk about
Who do you think Miriam ran to get?
The end of the story is in Exodus 2
verses 8 to 10.

A prayer to say
*Thank you, Father God, for helping
Miriam to keep Moses safe. Please
help me whenever you have a job for
me to do. Amen.*

The servant girl and the General

Bible reading: 2 Kings 5 verses 14 and 15
'Then Naaman's skin became new again … Naaman said, "Look. I now know there is no God in all the earth except in Israel."'

Thought for the day
General Naaman the brave, the strong, the famous army commander, had fallen ill with a dreadful skin disease. And in those days there was no cure. 'I know a cure,' said Naaman's wife's foreign servant girl. 'The man of God who lives in my country would cure the General.' And he did!

To talk about
Going to church is a way of showing that we are followers of Jesus. Are there any other ways?

A prayer to say
Dear Father God, General Naaman came to trust you, and all because of the servant girl. Thank you for helping her to obey you and speak up for you. Amen.

Parent power

Bible reading: Colossians 3 verse 20
'Children, obey your parents in all things. This pleases the Lord.'

Thought for today
I expect you do what your Mummy and Daddy tell you? They don't want you to get hurt or ill. That's why they sometimes say no to you. They love you, and so you trust them.

To talk about
What do you think is happening in today's picture?

A prayer to say
Dear Father God, thank you for my mum and dad who love me. Help me to do what they say without moaning. Amen.

APRIL 25

Just the same

**Bible reading: 1 Thessalonians 5
verses 17 and 18**
'Never stop praying. Give thanks whatever happens.
That is what God wants for you in Christ Jesus.'

Thought for today
For happy days and sad days, for sunshine and rain, for
good things and bad things, Thank you just the same.

To talk about
Can you finish this sentence: 'Prayer is asking God for things.
It's also saying t...y... to God. The answer is on April 7th.

A prayer to say
Please help me always to say thank you. Amen.

119

One came back

Bible reading: Luke 17 verse 16
'Then he bowed down at Jesus' feet and thanked him.'

Thought for today
There were once ten men who had a bad skin disease. When Jesus came past, they called out to him, 'Jesus, please help us!' And Jesus healed them all. But only one man thanked Jesus. Jesus said to him, 'Where are the other nine men?'

To talk about
Why do you think the men didn't thank Jesus?

A prayer to say
Dear Jesus, I'm sorry only one man came back to thank you. Help me to remember to say thank you to you and to everyone who looks after me when I'm ill. Amen.

APRIL 27

Grateful for my plateful

Bible reading: Genesis 1 verse 29

'God said, "Look, I have given you all the plants that have grain for seeds. And I have given you all the trees whose fruits have seeds in them. They will be food for you."'

Thought for today

In the time of Jesus, everyone said grace at mealtimes to thank God for their food. Jesus did, too (check it out - look at March 23rd). Today's prayer is an old Jewish grace, which Jesus himself may have used.

To talk about

Do you know the words of any graces that people say or sing today?

A prayer to say

Blessed be you, Lord God, who brings bread from the earth, and makes glad the hearts of your people. Amen.

APRIL 28

Winning words

Bible reading: 1 Corinthians 15 verse 57
'But we thank God! He gives us the victory through our Lord Jesus Christ.'

Thought for today

Tom was a wise man in his class nativity play. He asked Jesus to help him remember his part. Kim had been ill. Her teacher forgot to give her a part. She asked Jesus to help her not to mind. That night they both said thank you to Jesus.

To talk about

What do you like best - or least - about being in a play, or concert or class assembly?

A prayer to say

Dear Lord Jesus, thank you that with you I can win over my problems. Amen.

APRIL 29

Bang the drum

Bible reading: Psalm 92 verses 1 and 3
'It is good to praise the Lord, to sing praises to God Most High... to praise you with the ten-stringed lyre.'

Thought for today
Today's verse is from a Bible song. The Temple band played as the Temple choir sang these thank you words to God. Years later St Paul wrote, 'God takes care of us richly. He gives us everything to enjoy.' Can you make up a song to thank God for his love?

To talk about
What are your favourite musical instruments?

A prayer to say
Thank you, Lord God, for your goodness, your kindness and love. Amen.

APRIL 30

Jesus is the tops

**Bible reading:
2 Corinthians 9
verse 15**
'Thanks be to God for his gift that is
too wonderful to explain.'

Thought for today
St Paul wrote today's words, and he was
talking about Jesus. We've been
thinking about saying thank you to God
for all the things he's given us, and all
the ways he helps us. But most of all, we
thank him for sending Jesus.

To talk about
Do you have a favourite hymn about Jesus?

A prayer to say
*Dear Father God, thank you most of all for sending Jesus to this earth.
He became poor and died on the cross so that we can know your love.
Amen.*

Once upon a time

Bible reading: Genesis 2 verse 8
'Then the Lord God planted a garden in the East, in a place called Eden (which means Paradise).'

Thought for today
The garden that God made for Adam and Eve was a beautiful park. A crystal-clear river flowed through. Everywhere there were wild flowers and trees. The animals were not frightened. No sign said, 'Keep off the grass'.

To talk about
Is there a park near you?
What part do you like best?

A prayer to say
Thank you, Father God, for the gardens, parks and open spaces where I can play. Amen.

The two trees

Bible reading: Genesis 2 verse 9

'In the middle of the garden, God put the tree that gives life. And he put there the tree that gives the knowledge of good and evil.'

Thought for today

God used to talk with Adam and Eve in the garden. God said, 'You may eat the fruit from any tree in the garden, only you must not eat the fruit from the tree that gives the knowledge of good and evil. If you ever eat from that tree you will die.'

To talk about

Adam and Eve were gardeners. What job would you like to do when you grow up?

A prayer to say

Dear Father God, thank you because today I can hear your words in the Bible stories. Amen.

An evil angel

Bible reading: Genesis 3 verse 1
'One day the snake spoke to the woman.'

Thought for today
The snake was an evil angel. He said to Eve, 'Did God forbid you to eat fruit?' Eve said, 'If we eat fruit from that tree in the middle, we'll die.' 'No, you won't!' said the snake. 'You'll learn about good and evil. You'll be like God himself.' Will Eve believe God - or the snake?

To talk about
What should Eve have said to the snake?

A prayer to say
Dear Father God, help me never to listen to bad ideas, that go against what you say. Amen.

Deadly fruit

Bible reading: Genesis 3 verse 6

'The woman saw that the tree was beautiful. She saw that its fruit was good to eat and that it would make her wise.'

Thought for today

Oh dear! Eve fell for the snake's lies. She longed to taste the delicious-looking fruit, and she wanted to make herself wise. That's all she thought about. She picked the fruit and ate it. She gave some to Adam, too.

To talk about

Why didn't Eve ask God for his help?

A prayer to say

Dear heavenly Father, it's so sad that Eve took the fruit. It was stupid and wrong. Help me to do what's right. Amen.

MAY 5

Cowards

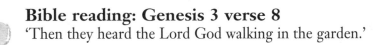

Bible reading: Genesis 3 verse 8
'Then they heard the Lord God walking in the garden.'

Thought for today
When Adam and Eve saw what they had done they were ashamed. They sewed fig leaves together to cover themselves. Then they heard God in the garden. What did they do? They ran away and hid among the trees.

To talk about
Is there something you would like God to help you not to do?

A prayer to say
Dear Father God, when I do something wrong, help me not to cover it up and hide, but to own up and say sorry. Amen.

MAY 6

'Don't blame me!'

Bible reading: Genesis 3 verse 9
'But the Lord God called to the man. The Lord said, "Where are you?"'

Thought for today
'I was hiding,' said Adam to God. 'Did you eat the forbidden fruit?' asked God. 'The woman gave it me,' said Adam. 'It was her fault. And you gave me the women.' 'What have you done?' God said to Eve. 'It was the snake's fault,' Eve said. 'He tricked me.'

To talk about
Adam blamed Eve. Who did he also blame?

A prayer to say
Dear Father God, when I do something wrong, help me not to blame it on someone else. Amen.

MAY 7

Thorns and thistles

Bible reading: Genesis 3 verses 14 to 15
'The Lord God said to the snake, "... Her child [descendant] will crush your head."'

Thought for today
After Adam and Eve rebelled against God, trouble came into the world. Thorns and thistles grew in the ground. The animals were wild and fierce. But God also made a promise. One day a child would be born who would destroy that evil angel and all its power.

To talk about
What are some of the bad things in the world today?

A prayer to say
Dear heavenly Father, thank you for sending Jesus. He did not give in to evil. He destroyed the power of the bad angel. Amen.

MAY 8

Mixed-up people

Bible reading: Romans 5 verses 12 and 19

'Sin came into the world because of what one man [Adam] did ... one man [Jesus] obeyed God, and many will be made right.'

Thought for today

When God first made Adam and Eve they were good. They loved one another and they loved God. But now the goodness was mixed up with badness. Sin and sadness had come into their lives and into the lives of all people born after them.

To talk about

Jesus was completely good. Can you remember some good things he did?

A prayer to say

Dear Father God, thank you for sending Jesus to make us completely good again. Amen.

MAY 9

Keep warm

Bible reading: Genesis 3 verse 21
'The Lord God made clothes from animal skins for the man and his wife.'

Thought for today
The beautiful world that God had made for Adam and Eve was all spoilt. But God still loved Adam and Eve. He made clothes for them to keep them warm.

To talk about
Which of your clothes do you most like wearing?

A prayer to say
Dear Father God, thank you because you are always kind and loving to us, even when we go against you. Amen.

A warning comes true

Bible reading: Genesis 3 verse 22

'God said, "Look ... the man knows good and evil. And now we must keep him from eating some of the fruit from the tree of life."'

Thought for today

Do you remember that there were two trees in the middle of the garden? One tree was the tree of life. Those who ate its fruit would live for ever. But to disobey God brought death (look back to May 2). So Adam and Eve had to leave the garden.

A prayer to say

Dear Father God, you had warned Adam and Eve that they would die if they ate the forbidden fruit. Help me to believe what you say. Amen.

To talk about

Do you know anyone who always keeps his or her promises?

A new home

Bible reading: Genesis 3 verse 23
'So the Lord God forced the man out of the garden of Eden. He had to work the ground.'

Thought for today
Adam and Eve had to make a new home and start all over again. They had enjoyed looking after the garden but from now on they had to grow their own food, and their work was hard and tiring.

To talk about
Jesus helps his friends to enjoy their work. What jobs do you like doing to help your mum and dad?

A prayer to say
Dear Father God, please help mummy and daddy with all the hard work they have to do. Amen.

A sword of fire

Bible reading: Genesis 3 verse 24

'Then God put angels on the east side of the garden. He also put a sword of fire there. It flashed around in every direction.'

Thought for today

Adam and Eve could never go back into the garden. It would be terrible for them to live for ever with sin in their lives. But when our bodies die, we can go to heaven and live for ever because Jesus takes away our sin.

To talk about

Where can people still eat fruit from the tree of life? (Answer in Revelation 2 verse 7, and 22 verse 2.)

A prayer to say

Dear Father God, thank you for sending Jesus to open the way for us to go to heaven. Amen.

Baby boys

**Bible reading:
Genesis 4 verse 1**
Eve said, 'With the Lord's help, I have given birth ...'

Thought for today
Adam gave his wife the name Eve, which means 'living'. After they left the garden, they had a baby boy they called Cain which means 'brought out', and then a baby boy called Abel which means 'breath'. The babies made Adam and Eve very happy.

To talk about
If you had a baby brother or sister, what names would you choose?

A prayer to say
*Thank you, heavenly Father, for helping Eve to have her babies.
And thank you for all new-born babies. Amen.*

MAY 14

Two ways

Bible reading: Isaiah 1 verse 17
'Learn to do good ...'

Thought for today
When we are very little, we do not understand the difference between good and bad. As we grow older, we know when something is wrong. When we do good things, we feel happy. Adam and Eve knew what was wrong and right and they chose to do wrong.

To talk about
Can you think of something to do that makes God happy?

A prayer to say
Heavenly Father, help me to do things that will make you and me happy. Amen.

May 15

Gimme! Gimme!

Bible reading: Hebrews 13 verse 5
'Be satisfied with what you have. God has said, "I will never leave you."'

Thought for today
God had given Adam and Eve so much: a beautiful garden, good food, happy work, their love for one another, and his love and presence with them. But they were not content: they wanted more.

To talk about
Think of five things that make you happy.

A prayer to say
Help me to trust you and my mummy and daddy to give me what I need. Help me to be happy with what I have. Amen.

MAY 16

Good gifts

Bible reading: Matthew 7 verse 11
'So surely your heavenly Father will give good things to those who ask him.'

Thought for today
Is there something you want very much? It might be a good thing, like wanting to see someone we love. We can ask our heavenly Father. He loves to give good gifts, and helps us to be patient if it's best for us to wait.

To talk about
Something you would very much like to have.

A prayer to say
Dear Father God, thank you because I can talk to you about the things I want. Amen.

Wise up

Bible reading: Genesis 3 verse 6
'She saw that its fruit ... would make her wise.'

Thought for today
Eve wanted to be wise. But to think that disobeying God makes you wise is stupid! Look back to January 6 to find out more about being wise.

To talk about
What does a wise person do? (Check it out: January 6.)

A prayer to say
Dear Father God, help me to be wise by obeying you. Amen.

MAY 18

Power mad

Bible reading: Genesis 3 verse 5

The snake said, 'If you eat the fruit from that tree, you will learn about good and evil. Then you will be like God.'

Thought for today

To be the best you can be for God - good. To think you're so clever you don't need God - bad! Eve wanted to eat the fruit to make herself big and important. She wanted power. She didn't want to please God!

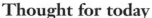

To talk about

What do conceited children do?

A prayer to say

Dear Father God, help me not to be big-headed. Help me to want to please you. Amen.

MAY 19

Pigs and copycats

Bible reading: Genesis 3 verse 6
'She took some of its fruit and ate it. She also gave some of the fruit to her husband, and he ate it.'

Thought for today
'Today I went to a party. I ate so much cake, I was sick. I gave some to my friends, and they ate so much it made them sick, too.'

To talk about
Can you think of any times when your friends have led you into trouble?

A prayer to say
Dear Father God, help me not to be greedy. And help me not to lead my friends into trouble. Amen.

Rules rule

Bible reading: Genesis 3 verse 3

Eve said, 'But God told us, "You must not eat fruit from the tree that is in the middle of the garden."'

Thought for today

In our land we have rules we call laws. There are laws to tell us how to keep safe on the roads, like a sign that tells drivers to stop. God has laws, too, called commandments. They are good laws that tell us all how to live safely and happily.

To talk about

Does your school have good rules?

A prayer to say

Dear heavenly Father, thank you for your rules that help us to live happily with one another. Amen.

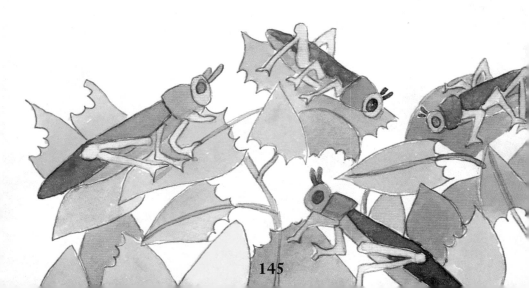

Millions of locusts

Bible reading: Joel 2 verses 28, 29 and 32
God said to Joel, 'I will give my Spirit freely to all kinds of people ... even to servants, both men and women ... Then anyone who asks the Lord for help will be saved.'

Thought for today
In Joel's time (before Jesus was born) God's Spirit came to only a few special people, not to everyone. Also, a terrible trouble had hit the land: millions of locusts were eating the crops. But God said, 'One day your troubles will end, and my Spirit will show my love to everyone who calls to me for help.'

To talk about
Do you have a problem you can ask God to help you with?

A prayer to say
Heavenly Father, thank you for your promise to Joel. Amen.

The wind blows

Bible reading: John 3 verse 8

Jesus said, 'The wind blows where it wants to go.
You hear the wind blow. But you don't know where
the wind comes from or where it is going. It is the same
with every person who is born from the Spirit.'

Thought for today

Can you see the wind? No, you can only see what it does. God's Holy
Spirit is like that. You can't see the Holy Spirit, but people who are on the
look-out see what he does.

To talk about

What do you like about the wind?

A prayer to say

*Thank you, heavenly Father, for the wind that shows us
about your Holy Spirit. Amen.*

MAY 23

Jesus from Nazareth

Bible reading:
Acts 10 verse 38
Peter said, 'You know about Jesus from
Nazareth. God ... [gave] him the Holy
Spirit and power. You know how Jesus
went everywhere doing good.'

Thought for today
After Joel (see May 21) many years went by.
Then Jesus came, full of God's Holy Spirit.
And now God wants to give his Holy Spirit
to people like you and me, children as well
as grown-ups, so that we can know God
and his love for us.

To talk about
Can you remember something good that
Jesus did?

A prayer to say
*Thank you, Father, for Jesus who showed
us your love. And thank you because you
want me to have your Holy Spirit.
Amen.*

MAY 24

Moving on

Bible reading: John 16 verse 7
Jesus said, 'If I do not go away, then the Helper will not come.'

Thought for today
Before he died, Jesus said goodbye to his friends. They wanted him to stay, but he had to go back to his Father in heaven. He said, 'Your hearts are filled with sadness ... But it is better for you that I go away. When I go away I will send the Helper to you.'

To talk about
The 'Helper' is one way of talking about the Holy Spirit.
Look back to January 24 to find another way.

A prayer to say
Heavenly Father, thank you for the Helper, the Holy Spirit. Amen.

MAY 25

God's guide

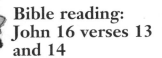

**Bible reading:
John 16 verses 13
and 14**

Jesus said to
his friends,
'But when
the Spirit of truth
comes, he will lead you
into all truth ... He will
take what I have to say
and tell it to you.'

Thought for today

When Jesus lived on earth, he gave his friends God's
teaching, and showed them how God wanted them to live.
Now Jesus was going away. But without Jesus, how would
his friends know what to do? Jesus said, 'Don't be
sad. The Spirit will teach and guide you.'

To talk about

How does Jesus describe the Spirit in today's verse?
What do you think this means?

A prayer to say

*Heavenly Father, I know you have
a plan for my life. Thank you
because your Spirit will guide
me and teach me. Amen.*

MAY 26

Waiting ...

Bible reading: Acts 1 verse 4

Jesus said to his friends, 'The Father has made you a promise ... Wait here [in Jerusalem] to receive this promise.'

Thought for today

Do you get excited when you've been promised something? Jesus promised the disciples that his Father would send them a present. This very special present was the Holy Spirit. They had to wait.

***

To talk about

Are you waiting for something special?

***

A prayer to say

Father God, sometimes, when I pray, I have to wait for you to answer my prayers. Please help me to be patient. Amen.

A roaring wind

Bible reading: Acts 2 verse 2

'Suddenly a noise came from heaven. It sounded like a strong wind blowing. This noise filled the whole house where they were sitting.'

Thought for today

It was Sunday morning, ten days after Jesus had gone back to his Father in heaven. Jesus' friends were waiting in a room in Jerusalem. They were praying and waiting. How would God send the present he had promised? Today's verse describes what suddenly happened.

To talk about

What are some of the best presents you've been given?

A prayer to say

Thank you, Father, because you always keep your promises. Amen.

Flames of fire

Bible reading: Acts 2 verses 3 and 4
'They saw something that looked like flames of fire. The flames were separated and stood over each person there. They were all filled with the Holy Spirit.'

Thought for today
As far as we know, the Holy Spirit did not come again with wind and fire. This was to mark the beginning of the church. Since then each of us who trusts Jesus is given the Holy Spirit to be our Helper and link us to Jesus.

To talk about
This day is the birthday of the church. What do you specially like about your birthday?

A prayer to say
Father, thank you for filling the disciples with your Spirit. Amen.

MAY 29

Break down the barriers

Bible reading: Acts 2 verse 11

Foreigners said, 'We hear these men telling in our own languages about the great things God has done.'

Thought for today

When the Holy Spirit came, the disciples wanted to tell everyone about Jesus. In Jerusalem there were many foreigners. Father God gave the disciples just what they needed. They found they were able to speak in other languages and could tell all the people, in their own languages, about God's love.

To talk about

The Holy Spirit made Jesus' friends brave; and broke the language barrier. How else does he help us?

A prayer to say

Thank you, Father God, because you want us to understand all that you have done for us. Amen.

MAY 30

'White Sunday'

Bible reading: Acts 2 verse 16
Peter said to the people in Jerusalem, 'Joel the prophet wrote about what is happening here today.'

Thought for today
When the people heard what God had done for them, and knew it was true, they asked, 'What shall we do?' Peter told them to be sorry for the things they had done wrong, to trust Jesus to forgive them, and be baptised. Then they would receive the gift of the Holy Spirit.

To talk about
In the past, new people joined the church on this day each year and wore new white clothes. What's your favourite colour to wear?

A prayer to say
'May the grace of the Lord Jesus Christ, the love of God, and the fellowship of the Holy Spirit be with us all.'
A prayer by St Paul

MAY 31

Power source

Bible reading: Acts 1 verse 8

Jesus said to his friends, 'The Holy Spirit will come to you. Then you will receive power. You will be my witnesses ...'

Thought for today

If a car has run out of petrol, how can I make it go? If I want to know and serve God, how can I please him? He gives us the power of his Holy Spirit to help us love and obey him.

To talk about

Don't forget, the Holy Spirit doesn't draw attention to himself. Who and what does he focus on?

A prayer to say

'Holy Spirit, help us,
Daily by your might,
What is wrong to conquer,
And to choose the right.'
By W H Parker

JUNE 1

Springtime

Bible reading: Luke 12 verse 32
Jesus said, 'Don't fear, little flock.'

Thought for today
In the spring the lambs skip and play in the fields. The ewes eat the grass and feed their baby lambs. The shepherd makes sure his sheep are safe. You are one of God's lambs, part of his little flock, and Jesus is your shepherd.

To talk about
In Bible times, why did a shepherd have to be brave? (Answer: look back to February 14.)

A prayer to say
Dear Lord Jesus, thank you for telling me not to be afraid. Thank you for keeping me safe. Amen.

June 2

Paid in full

Bible reading: Colossians 2 verse 14

'We owed a debt because we broke God's laws. That debt listed all the rules we failed to follow. But God forgave us that debt. He took away that debt and nailed it to the cross.'

Thought for today

In Bible times, people were often poor. Sometimes they owed money (called debts). If they couldn't pay they were thrown in prison. The wrong things we do are like debts we owe God. But God doesn't punish us because Jesus was punished instead. No one has to pay a debt twice over.

To talk about

Do you know any songs about Jesus dying for us?

A prayer to say

Dear Lord Jesus, thank you for your wonderful love. Thank you for taking the punishment instead of me. Amen.

The deepest sea

Bible verse: Micah 7 verse 19
'You will throw away all our sins into the
deepest sea.'

Thought for today
Some parts of the sea are so deep that no
one can reach the bottom. Anything that
falls down is lost for ever. The man who
wrote today's verse meant that God forgives
all our sins for ever.

To talk about
Something you've done wrong.
(God forgives you if you're sorry.)

A prayer to say
*Thank you, heavenly Father, that when you forgive our sins it's like
throwing them into the bottom of the deepest sea. Amen.*

June 4

Rubbed out

Bible reading: Isaiah 43 verse 25
God said, 'I, I am the One who forgives all your sins ... I will not remember your sins.'

Thought for today
When you rub out a mistake, what happens to it? Can you find it? When our heavenly Father forgives us for something we've done wrong, he never remembers it again.

To talk about
God forgets our sins - but we keep remembering them! Is there anything you keep on doing wrong?

A prayer to say
Dear heavenly Father, thank you for forgiving me for ... and thank you for forgetting all about it. Help me not to do it again. Amen.

JUNE 5

All ages

Bible reading: 1 John 2 verse 12

John said, 'I write to you, dear children, because your sins are forgiven through Christ.'

Thought for today

Whether we are big or little, we've all done wrong things. That's why Jesus died. When we're sorry for the wrong we've done, and ask God to forgive us, he does forgive us, because of Jesus.

To talk about

Do you remember how sin first came into the world? (Look back to May 4.)

A prayer to say

Dear heavenly Father, thank you for forgiving me. Amen.

Perfect love

Bible reading: 1 John 4 verse 19
'We love because God first loved us.'

Thought for today

Do you have aunts and uncles who say, 'My, how you've grown! I knew you when you were a baby!' Our heavenly Father knew us before we were born. He loved us then, and he still loves us. His love doesn't change according to how good we are.

To talk about

Something you like about your favourite aunt or uncle.

A prayer to say

Thank you, heavenly Father, because you loved me before I was born and you love me now. Amen.

161

JUNE 7

'That's all right!'

Bible reading: Ephesians 4 verse 32
'Forgive each other just as God forgave you in Christ.'

Thought for today
When we do wrong things, we make our heavenly Father sad. But if we say sorry, and mean what we say, what does our Father God do? (Look back to June 5.) Sometimes other people hurt us and make us sad. If they are sorry, what should we do?

To talk about
Has anybody made you sad, and then said sorry?

A prayer to say
Thank you, Father, for forgiving me.
Help me to forgive other people. Amen.

JUNE 8

The kind king

Bible reading: Matthew 18 verse 23
Jesus told a story about 'a king who decided to collect the money his servants owed him ...'

Thought for today
One of the servants owed his king millions of pounds.   'Sell all his things,' said the king. 'Please give me time to pay,' begged the servant. The king felt sorry for him. 'I'll let you off. You needn't pay anything,' said the king.   (Continued tomorrow)

To talk about
Jesus' stories always had two meanings. Who does the kind king remind you of? (Hint: look back to June 7.)

A prayer to say
Dear Father God, thank you because you are like that king. You forgive us all we have done wrong. Amen.

JUNE 9

Part 2: The wicked servant

Bible reading: Matthew 18 verse 28
'Later, that same servant found another servant who owed him a few pounds.'

Thought for today
Do you remember the servant we read about yesterday, the one who owed millions of pounds? A second servant owed that servant a few pounds. The first servant grabbed his neck. 'Pay me back.' 'Give me more time, please.' 'Impossible!' And he threw the second servant into prison.   (Continued tomorrow)

To talk about
What would you say to that wicked servant?

A prayer to say
Dear Father God, help me not to be nasty and mean to other people. Amen.

Part 3: A disgrace!

Bible reading: Matthew 18 verse 31
'All the other servants saw what happened.'

Thought for today
'Did you see what he did?' 'It's disgraceful!' The king's servants all went and told the king about that wicked servant. And the king was furious. He threw the wicked servant into prison. 'Stay there until you've paid back everything you owe,' he said.

-------- ⌒⌒⌒ --------
To talk about
Why was it right to report the wicked servant to the king?
---------- ⟡ ----------

A prayer to say
Dear Father God, we praise you because you are a great king. Everything you do is fair and good. Amen.

JUNE 11

Fair's fair

Bible reading: Matthew 18 verse 33
The king said, 'I had mercy on you. You
should have had the same mercy on that other
servant.'

Thought for today
We've seen that if we're sorry, God forgives us for the wrong things we do.
And if other people say sorry to us, we must forgive them. In the story of
the wicked servant Jesus shows us that if we refuse to forgive other people,
God cannot forgive us.

To talk about
Today's prayer is from the Lord's prayer. Can you see why some people
who pray that prayer are really saying, 'God don't forgive me'?

A prayer to say
*Dear Father God,
forgive the sins we
have done, just as
we forgive those
who did wrong to
us. Amen.*

June 12

False words and true feelings

Bible reading: Matthew 18 verse 35
Jesus said, 'Forgive your brother from your heart.'

Thought for today
Sometimes other children or grown-ups upset us. Then we say, 'It's all right,' but we don't really mean it. We still want to be cross. Jesus says we must really forgive other people, just as he really forgives us. He will help us if we ask him.

To talk about
Have you ever found it hard to forgive someone?

A prayer to say
Dear Father God, help me to truly forgive other people from my heart. Amen.

JUNE 13

Wham! Bam!

**Bible reading:
Colossians 3 verse 13**
'Do not be angry with each
other, but forgive each other.
If someone does wrong to
you, then forgive him.
Forgive each other because
the Lord forgave you.'

Thought for today
'He's wrong!' 'I'm right!' 'It's not fair!' 'Make her give it me!' Often we
quarrel and fight over things. But Jesus told us to give in to each other.

To talk about
What's happening in today's pictures?
Has something like this ever happened to you?

A prayer to say
*Dear Father God, I'm sorry when I fight and
quarrel and keep on wanting my own way.
Amen.*

JUNE 14

A billion, billion times

Bible reading: Matthew 18 verse 21

'Then Peter came to Jesus and asked, "Lord, when my brother sins against me, how many times must I forgive him? Should I forgive him as many as seven times?"'

Thought for today

What if someone goes on and on doing the same wrong thing, and saying sorry. What then? When can I stop forgiving him? And Jesus said to Peter, 'Forgive him 77 times.' That means, 'Forgive him a billion, billion times.'

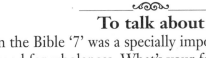

To talk about

In the Bible '7' was a specially important number. It stood for wholeness. What's your favourite number?

A prayer to say

Dear Father God, you never stop forgiving me. Thank you for your love for me. Amen.

JUNE 15

The four friends.

Bible reading: Mark 2 verse 2
'So many people gathered to hear Jesus preach that the house was full.
There was nowhere to stand, not even outside the door.'

Thought for today
The young man was paralysed. He had to lie flat on his back. One day his
friends rushed in. 'Quick!' they said, 'Jesus is back in town.' They lifted
their friend on to a stretcher and carried him to Jesus' home. But calamity!
At the house they couldn't get near Jesus. (Continued tomorrow)

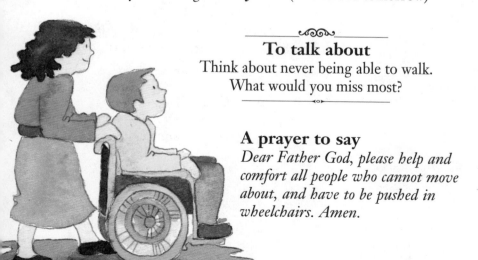

To talk about
Think about never being able to walk.
What would you miss most?

A prayer to say
*Dear Father God, please help and
comfort all people who cannot move
about, and have to be pushed in
wheelchairs. Amen.*

JUNE 16

Through the roof

Bible reading: Mark 2 verse 4
'So they went to the roof above Jesus.'

Thought for today
The friends had a bright idea! They climbed the stairs at the side of the house, and made a hole in the soft, flat roof. Inside the room, bits of dry mud and sticks fell on Jesus' head. He looked up - and there was a stretcher coming down! (Continued tomorrow)

To talk about
Have you ever been stuck with a problem, and then had a good idea?

A prayer to say
Dear Father God, thank you for giving the friends the idea of going on to the roof. Thank you that they kept going, and didn't give up. Amen.

JUNE 17

Winning faith

Bible reading: Mark 2 verse 5

'Jesus saw that these men had great faith. So he said to the paralysed man, "Young man, your sins are forgiven."'

Thought for today

Why did Jesus say that the man's sins were forgiven? Listen to today's verse again. After that Jesus said to the man, 'Stand up, take up your mat and walk.' And at once, in front of everybody, the man stood up.

To talk about

Someone you can pray for who is ill, or doesn't trust Jesus.

A prayer to say

Dear Lord Jesus, thank you for forgiving the man and healing him. I pray for ... Amen.

JUNE 18

Well-meaning and wrong-doing

Bible reading: Acts 26 verses 10 and 11
Paul said to the king, 'I did many things against God's people [the friends of Jesus]... I often punished them.'

Thought for today
Biddy wanted to help her mum. So in the garden she pulled up a lot of weeds. But her mum got cross. The weeds were really flowers! After Jesus had died, a man called Paul wanted to please God. So he tried to stop people being Christians! (Continued tomorrow)

To talk about
Have you ever tried to help someone, and ended up making things worse?

A prayer to say
Dear Father God, please help people today who are being punished and thrown into prison because they are Christians. Amen.

JUNE 19

A blinding light

Bible reading: Acts 26 verse 13
Paul said, 'I saw a light from heaven. The light was brighter than the sun.'

Thought for today
Saul travelled to Damascus, to find the Christians there, and throw them into prison. On the way, a bright light suddenly shone from the sky. Paul fell on the ground. A voice said, 'Why are you doing things against me?' Paul said, 'Who are you?' 'I am Jesus.'

To talk about
Someone you know or have heard of who tries to hurt Christians.

A prayer to say
Dear Lord Jesus, please help ... to start trusting in you. Amen.

JUNE 20

God's adventurer

Bible reading: Acts 26 verse 16
Jesus said to Paul, 'Stand up! I have chosen you ...'

Thought for today
Jesus forgave Paul for trying to hurt Christians. And he gave Paul a job to do. Paul had to tell people everywhere about Jesus and show them how to have their sins forgiven. Paul did what Jesus said, and had a great many adventures.

To talk about
What happened when Paul was in a shipwreck (see February 22).

A prayer to say
Dear Lord Jesus, thank you for forgiving Paul. Thank you for the way he obeyed you. Amen.

175

JUNE 21

Knock! Knock! Who's there?

Bible reading: Revelation 3 verse 20

'If anyone hears my voice and opens the door, I will come in and eat with him.'

Thought for today

Do you remember reading about picture language (January 2)? In today's verse each of us is compared to a house. Jesus is on the outside of our lives, knocking. He says, 'Can I come into your life, and stay with you, and be your friend?'

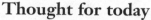

To talk about

In Bible times, sharing a meal was a sign of friendship. Today, how do you show you are friends with someone?

A prayer to say

Dear Lord Jesus, I want you to be my friend. Please come into my life, and stay with me. Amen.

176

Don't give up

Bible reading: Matthew 7 verses 7 and 8

Jesus said, 'Continue to ask, and God will give to you ... Everyone who continues asking will receive.'

Thought for today

If you asked your mum for some cake, she might say, 'It's nearly dinner time, don't spoil your appetite.' Our heavenly Father loves to give us gifts. But often he has a good reason to wait before answering our prayer. Keep on asking and trusting him, and don't give up.

To talk about

Look back at May 16. Did you receive what you asked for?

A prayer to say

Dear heavenly Father, help me not to give up, but to keep on talking to you about what I need. Amen.

June 23

Promises for keeps

Bible reading: Galatians 4
verses 4, 5 and 7
'But when the right time came, God sent his Son
... His purpose was to make us his children ... and God will give you what
he promised because you are his child.'

Thought for today
When we trust Jesus, God makes us his children (look back to February 13
and 16). What God promised is his forgiveness, love and friendship for
ever.

To talk about
What do you think is specially nice about
knowing you are God's child?

A prayer to say
*Dear Father God, thank you because
I know I am always
your child.
Amen.*

JUNE 24

What next?

Bible reading: Colossians 2 verse 6

Paul said, 'As you received Christ Jesus the Lord, so continue to live in him.'

Thought for today

It's your birthday, and you've been given a toy you've longed for. What do you do? a) Put it away and forget it? Or b) play with it? When you trust Jesus, and he becomes your friend, what should you do? a) Live in the way Jesus wants you to live? Or b) forget about him?

To talk about

How does Jesus want us to live?

A prayer to say

Dear Lord Jesus, help me not to forget about you. Amen.

JUNE 25

Go for gold

Bible reading: 1 Corinthians 9 verse 24

'You know that in a race all the runners run. But only one gets the prize. So run like that. Run to win!'

Thought for today

Ready, steady, go! The runners in a race run very hard because they want to win. Lose your determination, and you lose the race! Today's verse is using picture language. It means that if we want to see Jesus in heaven we must be determined. We must do our very best.

To talk about

What sports are you good at?

A prayer to say

Dear Lord Jesus, help me to do my best to trust and obey you. Amen.

June 26

A crown of glory

Bible reading: 1 Corinthians 9 verse 25
'All those who compete in the games use strict
training. They do this so that they can win a crown.
That crown is an earthly thing that lasts only a short time. But our crown
will continue for ever.'

Thought for today
When Paul was alive, winners in the Olympic Games were given a crown
made out of laurel leaves. Soon all the leaves withered away. In heaven,
Jesus will give each of us a reward - and it will last for ever. It's worth more
than any Olympic prize.

To talk about
What's the best prize or reward you've won?

A prayer to say
*Dear heavenly Father, thank you
that in heaven you will give me a
crown of glory that will never lose
its beauty. Amen.*

JUNE 27

The mighty marathon

Bible reading: Hebrews 12 verse 1
'So let us run the race that is before us and never give up.'

Thought for today
All Christians are running in a race. But our race is not a sprint (a short race), it's a marathon (a very, very long race). In a marathon, the great thing is not winning, but being brave enough to take part and finish the course.

To talk about
What type of races do you like best?

A prayer to say
Dear Father God, thank you for wanting me to take part in your race. Help me to keep going. Amen.

Love's proof

Bible reading: 1 John 4 verses 14 and 16
'We have seen that the Father sent his Son to be the Saviour of the world
... And so we know the love that God has for us, and we trust that love.'

Thought for today
How do we know that God loves us? The answer is in the first part of
today's verses. God will never let us down. In everything that happens he
works out his good plans for us.

To talk about
Listen to today's verses. What do you think
'Saviour of the world' means?

A prayer to say
*Heavenly Father, thank
you for sending Jesus.
Thank you for your
great love for us. I trust
you. Amen.*

JUNE 29

Attention! At ease!

Bible reading: Philippians 4 verse 7
'And God's peace will keep your hearts and minds in Christ Jesus.'

Thought for today
Outside a building, sentries are on guard duty. No enemy can come in. The people inside are safe. In today's verse the peace that God gives us is compared to a guard. If we pray about all our worries, and thank God for his help, we are safe.

To talk about
Look back to the talk about on January 25. What happened to your worry?

A prayer to say
Hurrah! Thank you because I don't have to worry any more. Amen.

Shifting shadows

Bible reading: James 1 verse 17
'God does not change like their shifting shadows.'

Thought for today

Shadows on the ground and on walls are always moving and changing. Other things change too: the weather changes and people change - their moods change and they change their minds. But God never changes and he always keeps his promises.

To talk about

Have you ever been let down by someone who didn't keep a promise? What happened?

A prayer to say

Dear Father God, thank you that you never change and your promises are always true. Amen.

185

JULY 1

A world turned bad

Bible reading: Genesis 6 verse 9
'Noah was a good man. He was the most
innocent man of his time.'

Thought for today
After Adam and Eve, many thousands of
years went by. A time came when all the people were mean, greedy, unkind
and cruel. All except for Noah. They thought God didn't know, or didn't
care or couldn't stop them. But they were wrong, as usual.

To talk about
Have you ever made a model that went wrong?
What did you do?

A prayer to say
*Dear heavenly Father, help us always to remember that you know and
you care when people do wrong things. Amen.*

July 2

God's plan

Bible reading: Genesis 6 verse 6
'God's heart was filled with pain.'

Thought for today
'I'm sorry I made these people,' God said to
Noah. 'I'm going to send a flood to rid my
world of them. But I will keep you and your
family safe. This is what you must do,' God
said. 'You must build a boat.'

To talk about
Can you remember another time when
someone made God very sad?
(Look back to May 3-5.)

A prayer to say
*Dear God, thank you
because you are
always fair and
good. You planned to
keep Noah safe.
Amen.*

JULY 3

A long box

Bible reading: Genesis 6 verse 15
God said, 'This is how big I want you to build the boat.'

Thought for today
God told Noah how to make the boat and they all set to work - Noah and his wife, and his sons, Shem, Ham and Japheth, and their wives. Noah's boat or ark (ark means box) was 450 feet long (longer than a football field), 45 feet high and 75 feet wide.

To talk about
What do you think Noah's neighbours said?

A prayer to say
Dear Father God, Noah's boat was shaped like a modern cargo ship. Thank you for such a safe floating home. Amen.

188

PLAN

Room for all

Bible reading: Genesis 6 verse 14
'Coat it inside and outside with tar.'

Thought for today
Noah's ark had three decks, and hundreds of little rooms, like nests.
To let in air, there was an opening all around the top of the boat, just
under the roof, which was probably flat, or slightly sloping. There was one
door. The tar was to make it waterproof.

ↄ໐໐໐

To talk about
What do you think all the little rooms were for?

A prayer to say
*Dear Father God, help me to be thoughtful and careful, like Noah.
Amen.*

July 5

A floating zoo

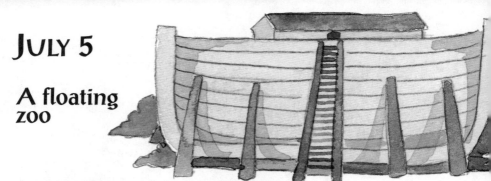

Bible reading: Genesis 6 verse 22
'Noah did everything that God commanded him.'

Thought for today
This is God's list of things to take:
> Seven pairs of every kind of 'clean' animal and bird ('clean' means they could be eaten); one pair of every kind of 'unclean' animal and bird, and food for everyone.

To talk about
What else do you think Noah took?
What would you take?

A prayer to say
Dear Father God, thank you for the way Noah obeyed you. Help me always to do what you want me to do. Amen.

JULY 6

All aboard

Bible reading: Genesis 7 verse 1
God said, 'You and your family go into the boat.'

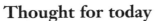

Thought for today
Two by two all the animals and birds and reptiles were taken into the little rooms in the ark. Then Noah and his family went in. Then God shut the door. The boat was still standing on dry land.

To talk about
What do you think the neighbours said now?

A prayer to say
Dear Father God, thank you for the way Noah and his family kept on obeying you. Amen.

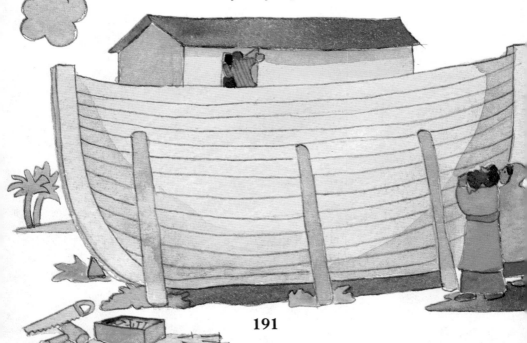

JULY 7

Torrents of rain

Bible reading: Genesis 7 verse 18
'The boat floated on the water above the earth.'

Thought for today
For seven days nothing happened. Then clouds covered the sky. Heavy rain began to fall. The river overflowed its bank. It was the flood. But Noah and his family and all the animals were safe. For 40 days and nights it rained solidly.

To talk about
What would be exciting about being on a boat?

A prayer to say
Thank you, Father God, for keeping Noah and his family safe. Please keep me and my family safe. Amen.

JULY 8

'Mud, mud, glorious mud'

Bible reading: Genesis 8 verse 1
'But God remembered Noah and all the wild animals and tame animals with him in the boat.'

Thought for today
After 40 days the rain stopped and slowly the water went down. One day Noah sent out a dove. It flew back with a leaf. After seven days Noah sent out the dove again and it didn't return. Noah took off the roof and looked out. There was thick, dry mud everywhere.

To talk about
The dove came back with a leaf - what did this mean?

A prayer to say
Dear heavenly Father, thank you because you didn't forget Noah, and you never forget me. Amen.

A rainbow promise

Bible reading: Genesis 8 verse 21
God said, 'I will never again destroy every living thing on the earth.'

Thought for today
God said, 'You can all come out!' They had been in the boat for 371 days. God put a rainbow in the clouds. He said, 'This is the sign of my agreement between me and you and every living thing.' And Noah and his family praised and thanked God.

To talk about
What does the rainbow remind us of?

A prayer to say
Dear Father God, thank you for the promise you made to Noah, and the new start you gave him. Amen.

July 10

Abram - the adventure starts

Bible reading: Genesis 12 verse 1

'Then the Lord said to Abram, "Leave your country, your relatives and your father's family. Go to the land I will show you."'

Thought for today

Many years after the flood, an old man called Abram lived in the town of Haran, where everyone worshipped the moon. When Abram was 75 God gave him an amazing command: listen to today's verse again. Abram trusted God and with his wife, Sarah, and his nephew, Lot, he set off.

To talk about

An adventure you've had.

A prayer to say

Father God, thank you because we are never too old or too young for you to speak to us. Amen.

JULY 11

The promised land

Bible reading: Genesis 12 verse 7
The Lord said to Abram, ' I will give this land to your descendants.'

Thought for today
With their donkeys, their sheep, their goats, their tents and their servants, Abram, Sarah and Lot travelled to the land of Canaan. And there God said to Abram, 'This is the land. I'm giving it to you and your descendants.'

To talk about
What do you like about sleeping in a tent?

A prayer to say
Dear heavenly Father, help me to trust your promises, as Abram did. Amen.

July 12

Servants' squabbles

Bible reading: Genesis 13 verses 14 and 15

'After Lot left, the Lord said to Abram, "Look all around you ... All this land that you see I will give to you and your descendants for ever."'

Thought for today

'We need that water.' 'No, this is our well.' 'Go away.' There was not enough grass and water to go round, so Abram's and Lot's servants were fighting. 'We mustn't quarrel,' said Abram to Lot. 'We'll separate. You take first choice.' Lot chose a rich, well-watered part of the country.

To talk about

A fight or quarrel you've had. What was it about? How did it end?

A prayer to say

Dear heavenly Father, Abram didn't grab the best for himself. Help me to be like him. Amen.

Abram to the rescue

Bible reading: Genesis 14 verse 15

'That night Abram divided his men into groups. And they made a surprise attack against the enemy.'

Thought for today

The lovely land Lot chose was not lovely at all. Wicked and warlike people were living there. In a battle with enemy kings, Lot and his family were carried off as prisoners. As soon as he heard, Abram chased after them with his servants and rescued Lot and his family.

To talk about

Lot made a wrong choice. Has that ever happened to you?

A prayer to say

Dear Father God, help me, as I grow up, to stand up for people who are attacked or bullied. Amen.

JULY 14

Star-gazing

Bible reading: Genesis 15 verse 5
'God said, "Look at the sky. There are so many stars you cannot count them. And your descendants will be too many to count."'

Thought for today
Abram was really old now, and still he hadn't any children. He prayed about this, and God promised him more descendants than stars in the sky! 'Descendants' means great-grandchildren, and great-great-grandchildren, and so on and on into the future. And Abram believed God.

To talk about
Something that makes you sad.

A prayer to say
Thank you, Father God, because Abram talked to you when he was sad. Amen.

199

JULY 15

Father Abraham

Bible reading: Genesis 17 verse 6
God said to Abram, 'Kings will come from you.'

Thought for today
Abram was now 99 and Sarah was 90 and still they didn't have a son. God said, 'I will give you a new name. You will be called Abraham.' This means 'Father of many nations'. Abraham kept on believing God. And God's promise came true. Abraham became the ancestor of all Arabs and Jews.

To talk about
Does your name have a meaning?

A prayer to say
Dear Father God, thank you because you always do what you say. Amen.

200

July 16

Something to laugh about

Bible reading: Genesis 18 verse 12
'Sarah laughed to herself, "My husband and I are too old to have a baby."'

Thought for today
Do you remember the mysterious visitors who came out of the desert? (see February 25). This was their message: 'Sarah will have a son.' Sarah, who was eavesdropping in her tent, didn't believe them. Then the next year Isaac was born.

To talk about
Isaac's name means 'he laughs'.
Why do you think Sarah gave him this name?

A prayer to say
Heavenly Father, help us to remember that nothing is too hard for you. Amen.

Slave labour

Bible reading: Exodus 1 verse 11

'The Egyptians made life hard for the people of Israel. They put slave masters over the Israelites.'

Thought for today

Baby Moses, hidden in the reeds by the river, grew up to be a prince of Egypt. But his own people, the Israelites, were forced to work in slave labour gangs. When he was grown up, Moses ran away from the palace, and became a shepherd.

To talk about

Do you remember how baby Moses was saved from being murdered?

A prayer to say

Heavenly Father, please help all people who are suffering because other people are cruel, greedy and unfair. Amen.

Bible reading: Exodus 3 verse 7
'The Lord said, "I have seen the troubles my people have suffered in Egypt."'

Thought for today

Forty years passed by. One day, Moses was with his sheep when he saw a bush, all on fire, but not burning up. He went closer, and out of the flames God spoke. 'I am sending you to Pharaoh,' God said. 'Go! Bring my people out of Egypt.'

To talk about

Do you know of anyone who tries to help suffering people in the world today?

A prayer to say

Heavenly Father, you still tell men and women to go and help poor, sick and suffering people. Please especially help ... Amen.

March free

Bible reading: Exodus 12 verse 33
'The Egyptians also asked the Israelites to hurry and leave.'

Thought for today
'I will certainly not let the slaves go!' Pharaoh was furious. How dare Moses make this ridiculous request! But Moses didn't give up, and at last, after many troubles, Pharaoh said, 'Yes. Go! At once!' So Moses led the slaves out into the desert.

To talk about
Have you ever tried to do something, and failed, and kept on trying, like Moses?

A prayer to say
Heavenly Father, thank you for giving Moses the courage to rescue his people. Amen.

Don't panic!

Bible reading: Exodus 14 verses 5, 6, and 8
Pharaoh said, '"What have we done ... We have lost our slaves." So the king prepared his war chariot and took his army with him ... he chased the Israelites.'

Thought for today
In the desert the Israelites camped by an inland sea. Suddenly they saw clouds of dust. Chariots! 'God will rescue you,' Moses said. He held up his staff. And God sent a wind which drove aside the water and made a pathway. When everyone had crossed, the waters flowed back.

To talk about
Make up a victory song for Moses.
(The song Moses made up is in Exodus15.)

A prayer to say
Moses said, 'Don't be afraid. You need only to remain calm. The Lord will fight for you.' Thank you for these words. Amen.

July 21

The Ten Commandments

Bible reading: Exodus 19 verses 3 and 5
God said, 'Tell this to the people of Israel ... obey me ... and you will be my own possession.'

Thought for today
Moses led the people to God's holy mountain, called Sinai. They made camp in the foothills, and Moses climbed the mountain. There God gave Moses ten commandments. Here are four: Do not worship any other god. Do not steal. Do not tell lies. Treat your parents with respect.

To talk about
Pretend that you and 20 other people are stranded on a desert island. Work out some rules that everyone must keep.

A prayer to say
Thank you, Father God, for your rules, which show us the right way to live. Amen.

JULY 22

God's choice

Bible reading: 1 Samuel 16 verse 7
'People look at the outside of a person, but God looks at the heart.'

Thought for today
Moses died, and many years went by. 'Quick, you're wanted at the farm,' a servant said. David, a shepherd boy, rushed home. He saw his father and his brothers looking puzzled. Samuel, an old prophet, said, 'God has chosen you, David.'

To talk about
Why didn't Samuel choose one of David's big brothers? Today's verse gives the answer.

A prayer to say
Heavenly Father, you see what I am thinking and feeling, and you know all about me, just as you knew about David and his brothers.
Amen.

207

July 23

Trembling in terror

Bible reading: 1 Samuel 17 verse 21
'The Israelites and Philistines were lining up their men to face each other in battle.'

Thought for today
David was to be king - but not yet. It was a secret. Enemies were attacking David's country, and David's brothers had gone to join the war. 'Take this food to your brothers,' said David's dad, 'and see how they are.' At the battle lines the Israelites were trembling in terror.

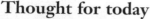

To talk about
'I want you to go on an errand.' If your teacher said that to you, would you be glad or worried?

A prayer to say
Dear heavenly Father, whenever I feel frightened, help me to remember to pray to you for help. Amen.

A dare

Bible reading: 1 Samuel 17 verse 10
Goliath said, 'Today I stand and dare the army of Israel. Send one of your men to fight me.'

Thought for today
The Israelites were camped on a hill, the enemy were on the opposite hill. In the middle was a valley. Every day an enemy warrior strode forward. He was Goliath, a great giant of a man. 'I challenge you to a fight,' he roared. 'Whoever wins, wins the war.'

To talk about
'Go on, I dare you!' Have you ever heard anyone say that to someone? What happened?

A prayer to say
Thank you, Father, that even in front of giants we can trust you. Amen.

JULY 25

Cowards, a fool and a hero

Bible reading: 1 Samuel 17 verse 26
David said, 'Why does Goliath think he can speak against the armies of the living God?'

Thought for today
'You're a bunch of cowards,' Goliath jeered. 'He's in for a nasty shock,' David said. 'God's on our side. You can't beat God.' David's brother heard him. 'Cheeky!' he said. 'Clear off home to those few sheep.' 'I'll fight Goliath,' David said to King Saul.

To talk about
Why was David's brother so nasty to David?

A prayer to say
Heavenly Father,
thank you for
David's courage
and trust in you.
Amen.

Down and out

Bible reading: 1 Samuel 17 verses 46 and 47
David said, 'All the world will know there is a God in Israel ... The battle belongs to him!'

Thought for today
David took his sling, and five smooth, round stones. He walked towards Goliath. Goliath snarled at David. 'I'll make mincemeat of you.' David put a stone in his sling, and whirled it round his head. Out it whizzed, right into Goliath's forehead. That was the end of Goliath.

To talk about
Do you know any stories about giants?

A prayer to say
Dear Father God, you have enemies today. Help me to trust you, and stand up for you. Amen.

July 27

King David

Bible reading: 2 Samuel 8 verse 15
'David was king over all Israel. His decisions were fair and right for all his people.'

Thought for today
David's friend, Jonathan, died in battle. Later, King David said, 'Is there anyone still left in Saul's family? I want to show kindness for Jonathan's sake.' 'Yes,' a servant said, 'Jonathan has a crippled son.'
So Jonathan's son came to live in the palace with King David's family.

To talk about
Would you like to be a king or queen or president?

A prayer to say
Heavenly Father, please help all rulers. Give them kindness and wisdom to make fair and right decisions. Amen.

July 28

Dance music

Bible reading: 1 Samuel 29 verse 5
'David is the one the Israelites sings about in their dances: "Saul has killed thousands of his enemies. But David has killed tens of thousands."'

Thought for today
David became King Saul's helper, and played music to soothe him when he felt ill. David became best friends with Saul's son, Jonathan. When he was grown up, David was a brave soldier and great army leader. After Saul and Jonathan died, David was crowned king.

To talk about
Today's verse was a pop song in David's time. What's your favourite pop song?

A prayer to say
Thank you for brave David. Amen.

A shepherd's song

Bible reading: Psalm 23 verses 1 and 2
'The Lord is my shepherd. I have everything I need. He gives me rest in green pastures. He leads me to calm water.'

Thought for today
When David was a boy he looked after his father's sheep. He led them to grassy places on the rocky mountain sides; he took them to streams of clear water. Today's verse is from a song that David himself wrote.

To talk about
Sing a song about God looking after us.

A prayer to say
Thank you, Lord Jesus, because you give me all I need. You are my loving shepherd. Amen.

July 30

Stuck!

Bible reading: Psalm 23 verse 4
'I will not be afraid because you are with me. Your rod and your staff comfort me.'

Thought for today
Sheep are silly creatures. Sometimes they wander off by themselves. They get caught in brambles or fall down cliffs. David's long shepherd's staff was curved at one end. With his staff he hooked away brambles, and pulled his sheep up from crevices.

To talk about
As well as a staff and rod, a shepherd had a sling. What do you think that was for?

A prayer to say
Dear Lord Jesus, thank you because I know you are with me to help me when I'm in any kind of trouble. Amen.

July 31

Sweet dreams

**Bible reading:
John 10 verse 7**
'Jesus said, "I tell you the truth. I am the door for the sheep."'

Thought for today
In the summer the shepherd often stayed out all night in the hills with his sheep. At night, to keep his sheep together and safe from wild animals and robbers, he would make a sheepfold out of rocks and brambles. Instead of a door, the shepherd himself would lie across the entrance.

To talk about
What helps you to go to sleep at night?

A prayer to say
Dear Lord Jesus thank you for saying you are like the door of the sheepfold. Each night, as I go to sleep, help me to remember that you are guarding me. Amen.

AUGUST 1

Prisoners

Bible reading: Daniel 1 verse 3
'He wanted [the young men] to be from important families. And ... from the family of the king of Judah.'

Thought for today
In the year 605BC King Nebuchadnezzar marched to Jerusalem. He captured the city, looted the temple, and took the king prisoner. 'Choose the best

young men from the best families,' King Nebuchadnezzar said to his chief officer. 'Choose young men who are good-looking, healthy and clever, and enrol them in my palace school in Babylon.'

To talk about
It must have been sad to leave Jerusalem, but exciting to go to another country.
What countries would you like to travel to?

A prayer to say
Dear Father God, please help all people who are working to stop wars in the world today. Amen.

August 2

Forbidden food

Bible reading: Daniel 1 verse 6
'Among those young men were some from the people of Judah [Jerusalem]. These were Daniel, Hananiah, Mishael and Azariah.'

Thought for today
The cleverest young men from all over the Babylonian empire were students in the king's school in Babylon. They were served rich food and wine from the king's own table. 'This food and wine has been offered to idols,' Daniel said. 'If we eat it, we'll be breaking God's law.'

To talk about
Daniel had to learn the Babylonian language. What foreign languages would you like to learn?

A prayer to say
Dear Father God, thank you for the way Daniel obeyed you, even in a foreign school in a strange land. Amen.

August 3

Health food

Bible reading: Daniel 1 verse 7
'Daniel's new name was Belteshazzar.
Hananiah's was Shadrach. Mishael's was
Meshach. And Azariah's new name was Abednego.'

Thought for today
'If you don't eat properly, you'll get ill, and then the king will cut off my
head,' said Ashpenaz, the chief officer. 'Judge for yourself,' said Daniel to
the guard. 'For ten days give us only vegetables and water.' After ten days
Daniel and his friends were more healthy than all the other students!

To talk about
What's your favourite vegetable?

A prayer to say
*Thank you, heavenly Father, for Daniel's guard
who was fair and understanding. Please help
all prison guards and officers. Amen.*

AUGUST 4

Star pupils

**Bible reading:
Daniel 1 verse 20**
The king found out that
'they were ten times
better than all the
fortune-tellers and
magicians in his
kingdom.'

Thought for today
After three years, when
it was time for the final
exams, Daniel and his friends came top of the class! Then King
Nebuchadnezzar ordered Daniel, Shadrach, Meshach and Abednego to
join his team of wise men, magicians and astrologers.

To talk about
What do you find hardest to do at school?

A prayer to say
*Thank you, heavenly Father,
for my school and the help you
give me to learn. Please help
me with ... Amen.*

August 5

Magicians in a mess

Bible reading: Daniel 2 verse 18
'Daniel asked his friends to pray to the God of heaven.'

Thought for today
One day King Nebuchadnezzar summoned his magicians and fortune-tellers. 'I've had a dream. Tell me what it was.'
'O King live for ever - what you're asking is too hard.'

'They're useless. Kill them.'
But God told Daniel the dream, and its meaning, and no one was killed.

To talk about
A dream you've had.

A prayer to say
'Praise God for ever and ever. He gives wisdom to people. I thank and praise you. You told us about the king's dream.' (This is part of Daniel's thank you prayer)

221

AUGUST 6

Top jobs

**Bible reading:
Daniel 2 verse 48**
And the king 'put
Daniel in charge of all
the wise men of
Babylon.'

**Thought for
today**
King Nebuchadnezzar
was so pleased that
Daniel was able
to tell him about
his dream that he
gave Daniel many presents and made
him ruler over the whole area of
Babylon. Daniel asked the king if his
friends, Shadrach, Meshach and Abednego, could help him
and the king said yes.

To talk about
What are some important and difficult jobs people have today?

A prayer to say
*Dear Father God, please help Christians who
have important jobs to do. Amen.*

AUGUST 7

Horns, harps and tambourines

Bible reading: Daniel 3 verse 12
'They do not serve your gods, and they do not worship the gold statue you set up.'

Thought for today
King Nebuchadnezzar set up a tall, gold statue. He said to the people, 'When the music plays, bow down and worship the statue. Anyone who refuses will be thrown into the blazing furnace.'

Spies came to King Nebuchadnezzar. 'O King, Shadrach, Meshach and Abednego will not bow down.

To talk about
Why wouldn't Shadrach, Meshach and Abednego bow down to the statue?

A prayer to say
Heavenly Father, help me to be brave like Shadrach, Meshach and Abednego. Amen.

223

Idol threats

Bible reading: Daniel 3 verse 18
'We want you, our king, to know this: we will not serve your gods.'

Thought for today

'Worship my statue,' the king shouted at Shadrach, Meshach and Abednego, 'or die in the fire. No God can save you from my power.'

But the friends said, 'The God we serve is able to save us. But even if he does not, we will not worship the statue.'

To talk about

People don't worship gold statues today. But what do they often worship (think about all the time)?

A prayer to say

Heavenly Father, even when things seem to go badly, help me to trust you. Amen.

In the furnace

Bible reading: Daniel 3 verse 25
'The fourth man looks like a son of the gods.'

Thought for today
'Heat up my furnace seven times hotter than usual,' screamed the king.
King Nebuchadnezzar sat and watched while soldiers tied up Shadrach,
Meshach and Abednego and threw them into the flames. Suddenly the
king jumped up. 'I can see four men and they're walking around in the
fire.'

To talk about
What happened to Daniel when he
wouldn't stop praying to God?
(See February 26.)

A prayer to say
*Father God, thank you because you
are for real. Amen.*

225

A smoke-free zone

Bible reading: Daniel 3 verse 28
'Then Nebuchadnezzar said, "Praise the God of Shadrach, Meshach and Abednego. Their God has sent his angel and saved his servants from the fire."'

Thought for today
'Come on out,' King Nebuchadnezzar called to Shadrach, Meshach and Abednego. Everyone crowded around them. Their hair was not scorched, their clothes were not burned, they didn't even smell of smoke. Then the king made a new law: no one must say anything against the God of Shadrach, Meshach and Abednego.

To talk about
Can you remember how David proved that there is a God who saves?
(Look back to July 26.)

A prayer to say
Thank you, Father God, for saving Shadrach, Meshach and Abednego. Amen.

August 11

'Gimme my share!'

Bible reading: Luke 15 verse 11
'Then Jesus said, "A man had two sons."'

Thought for today
This is a story Jesus told. It's about a young man who thought his life would be better without his parents. Then he learned that it was his father's love that had given him all he had. He was the youngest son, and he wanted to get away and enjoy himself.

To talk about
Some stories you like.

A prayer to say
Father God, you are our heavenly Father. In your love you give us everything to enjoy. Amen.

227

AUGUST 12

Looking for the good time

Bible reading: Luke 15 verse 12
'So the father divided the property between his two sons.'

Thought for today
'Please, Dad, can I have the money now that I would get when you die?' This made the father very sad. But he gave his son the money to go and spend how he wanted. Then the young man packed his bags and left home.

To talk about
Some nice things about your home.

A prayer to say
Father God, please help me to be content with what I have and not to want more. Amen.

AUGUST 13

Empty pockets

Bible reading: Luke 15 verse 14
'There was not enough food to eat anywhere in the country.'

Thought for today
The young man went off to a distant country, and there he wasted all his money on all sorts of wrong things. Then there was no rain and the harvest failed. He had no money left so he got a job on a farm feeding the pigs.

To talk about
What do you think of the younger son?

A prayer to say
Heavenly Father, thank you for my home and family and friends. Amen.

AUGUST 14

Poorer than a pig

Bible reading: Luke 15 verse 16
'No one gave him anything.'

Thought for today
The people listening to this story thought that looking after pigs was a disgusting job. It was against their law. This young man, said Jesus, was so hungry that he even wanted to eat the pigs' food!

To talk about
If Jesus were telling this story today, what job do you think he would give the younger son?

A prayer to say
Heavenly Father, that son was learning the hard way! Please help me to listen to people who love me. Help me not to do things that will harm me. Amen.

Straight thinking

Bible reading: Luke 15 verse 18
The son said, 'I will leave and return to my father.'

Thought for today
'I've been such a fool!' the son said. 'What am I doing here? My father's servants have plenty to eat, while here I am, starving. I'll go back to my father and ask him to forgive me, and beg him to take me on as one of his servants.'

To talk about
What did the younger son do that was wrong?

A prayer to say
Heavenly Father, please forgive me when I do wrong things. Amen.

The home-coming

Bible reading: Luke 15 verse 21
'The son said, "Father, I have sinned against God and have done wrong to you. I am not good enough to be called your son."'

Thought for today
The father longed for his son to come back. He would stand and stare into the distance, waiting to see him. And one day, there he was, a far-off figure. The father felt sorry for his son. He ran to him, hugged him and kissed him.

To talk about
Jesus' stories always had a hidden meaning. What do you think this story means?

A prayer to say
Father God, thank you that you are always there, waiting for me to be sorry, and you always say, 'It's all right. I forgive you.' Amen.

AUGUST 17

Party time

Bible reading: Luke 15 verse 24
The father said, 'My son was dead, but now he is alive again!
He was lost, but now he is found.'

Thought for today
'Quick,' the father said to the servants. 'Get his best clothes,
and sandals, and a signet ring, and put them on him.' (Sandals
showed he was a son: slaves went barefoot.) That night the
father held a great feast, with music and dancing, for his son
who was found again.

To talk about
How does your family celebrate good news?

A prayer to say
*Dear Lord Jesus, thank you for your story, which
shows how much you love us. Amen.*

AUGUST 18

A lost coin

Bible reading: Luke 15 verses 3 and 8
'Jesus told them this story ... "Suppose a woman has ten silver coins, but she loses one of them.'

Thought for today
In the time of Jesus, after a young lady was married, she wore a circlet of ten silver coins as a head dress. These coins were precious, like the jewels in an engagement ring. When Jesus told today's story, he may have been thinking of these coins.

To talk about
Where do you keep your jewellery or precious things?

A prayer to say
Dear Lord Jesus, thank you because you understand how bad we feel when we lose things. Amen.

August 19

Hunt the coin

Bible reading: Luke 15 verse 8

Jesus said, 'She will light a lamp and clean the house. She will look carefully for the coin until she finds it.'

Thought for today

There were no electric lights in the time of Jesus, and a room had only one very small window, so it was dark. Floors were ordinary earth, perhaps spread with dried reeds. The woman got her broom, and swept the floor very carefully as she searched for her coin.

A prayer to say
Dear Lord Jesus, thank you because you never give up on us. Amen.

To talk about
Did the woman say, 'It's no use! I give up!'? (Listen to today's verse again.)

235

Great news

Bible reading: Luke 15 verse 10
Jesus said, 'There is joy before the angels of God when one sinner changes his heart.'

Thought for today
'I've found it! I've found my coin!' The woman dashed out of her house and told all her friends. And they were as glad as she was.

There's a hidden meaning to this story. People who ignore Jesus, and go against him, are like that lost coin.

To talk about
In the story, who is very happy? Who else is very happy - listen to today's verse.

A prayer to say
Dear Lord Jesus, thank you because you and all the angels of heaven are so happy when someone starts loving you and trusting you.
Amen.

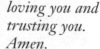

AUGUST 21

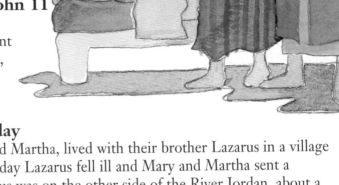

An urgent message

Bible reading: John 11 verse 3
'Mary and Martha sent someone to tell Jesus, "Lord, the one you love is sick."'

Thought for today
Two sisters, Mary and Martha, lived with their brother Lazarus in a village called Bethany. One day Lazarus fell ill and Mary and Martha sent a message to Jesus. Jesus was on the other side of the River Jordan, about a day's journey away.

To talk about
Who can you pray for today?

A prayer to say
Dear Lord Jesus, please may ... feel better soon. Amen.

AUGUST 22

Waiting

Bible reading: John 11 verse 4
'Jesus said, "This sickness will not end in death. It is for the glory of God."'

Thought for today
When the message came, Jesus waited for two days. Then he said, 'Our friend Lazarus has fallen asleep.'

Jesus' friends said, 'That's good. He'll get better now.'

But Jesus said, 'Lazarus has died. I'm glad I wasn't there because this will help you believe. We'll go to him now.'

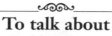

To talk about
A time when God hasn't seemed to answer your prayers.

A prayer to say
Dear Lord Jesus, I always want you to answer my prayers straight away. When you don't seem to answer, help me to believe that you have a good reason. Amen.

AUGUST 23

If only

Bible reading: John 11 verse 25
Jesus said to Martha, 'I am the resurrection and the life.
He who believes in me will have life even if he dies.'

Thought for today
When Jesus came to Bethany, Lazarus had been in the tomb for four days.
Martha heard that Jesus was coming and hurried out to meet him. 'If you
had been here, my brother would not have died,' she said.

'Lazarus will live again,' Jesus said.

To talk about
Something you feel or have felt angry or upset about. (Martha and Mary
were honest with Jesus about their feelings.)

A prayer to say
*Dear Lord Jesus, thank you
because when we trust you we
live with you for ever. Amen.*

AUGUST 24

Deep sadness

Bible reading: John 11 verse 33
'Jesus felt very sad in his heart and was deeply troubled.'

Thought for today
Martha hurried back to Mary. 'Jesus is asking for you,' Martha said. So Mary ran to see Jesus.

'He would not have died if you had been here,' Mary said. Jesus saw Mary and other people with her, all crying. And Jesus cried, too.

To talk about
When you are sad, what helps you?

A prayer to say
Dear Lord Jesus, thank you because when I am sad you understand how I feel. Amen.

Roll back the stone

Bible reading: John 11 verse 40

Jesus said to Martha, 'Didn't I tell you that if you believed, you would see the glory of God?'

Thought for today

Lazarus was buried in a cave, with a large stone in front of the entrance. They went to the cave. 'Move the stone away,' Jesus said. Jesus prayed and then he called, 'Lazarus, come out!' And out came Lazarus - alive! When they saw this, many people believed.

To talk about

Who else was buried in a cave with a stone in front? (Look back to March 21.)

A prayer to say

Dear Lord Jesus, we praise you because you brought Lazarus back to life, and everybody saw your power and love. Amen.

AUGUST 26

Happy talk

Bible reading: John 16 verse 24

Jesus said, 'You have never asked for anything in my name. Ask and you will receive. And your joy will be the fullest joy.'

Thought for today

When we pray, will we get anything we ask for? No! Look at today's verse. God says 'yes' to prayers made 'in the name of Jesus'. This means prayers that are Christ-like, the type of prayers that Jesus would pray, and that match what he wants for us.

To talk about

What do you think is the wrong sort of prayer?

A prayer to say

Dear heavenly Father, thank you because you answer prayers asked in the name of Jesus, and you want us to have the fullest joy. Amen.

AUGUST 27

For ever friends

Bible reading: John 3 verse 15
'Then everyone who believes in him can have eternal life.'

Thought for today
You are a person. You feel happy or sad or scared. You eat and drink, and sleep. You love; you think; you choose to do good or bad things. Eternal life means living for ever with Jesus as your close friend. When your body dies, God will give you a new, perfect body.

To talk about
How do we have eternal life? (Listen to today's verse again.)

A prayer to say
Thank you, God, for making me me, Amen.

A gift

Bible reading: Ephesians 2 verse 8
'You did not save yourselves. It was a gift from God.'

Thought for today

God wants to give you a present - you, and all grown-ups and children everywhere. To get this present we don't have to be good, or do anything except ask. The present is being able to trust Jesus. When we do, we are 'saved'. That means, God gives us the gift of eternal life (look back to yesterday).

To talk about

Who is Jesus? (Turn to January 12.)

A prayer to say
Jesus, friend of little children
Be a friend to me.
Take my hand and ever keep me
Close to thee. Amen.
by W. J. Mathams

At ease!

Bible reading: Philippians 4 verse 7
'And God's peace will keep your hearts and minds in Christ Jesus. The peace that God gives is so great that we cannot understand it.'

Thought for today
Do you know what peace means? It means being quiet and calm, and not being worried or afraid. It means feeling at ease. It means knowing that God loves you and forgives you. It means loving other people and not fighting with them.

To talk about
In today's verse, the word 'keep' means 'guard', like a soldier. What can you now stop worrying about or being afraid of?

A prayer to say
Dear Father God,
thank you for your
gift of peace.
Amen.

AUGUST 30

Jesus prays

Bible verse: John 17 verse 24

Jesus said, 'Father, I want those you have given me ... to see my glory. This is the glory you gave me because you loved me before the world began.'

Thought for today

Imagine Jesus sitting on a great throne, wearing beautiful clothes and shining with light. If we love Jesus and go to live with him, we will see him in all his glory.

To talk about

Do you remember something that Jesus is doing in heaven?
(See March 28.)

A prayer to say

Jesus, you are wonderful and glorious. Amen.

AUGUST 31

Mysteries

Bible reading: John 14 verse 26
Jesus said, 'But the Helper will teach you everything ... This Helper is the Holy Spirit whom the Father will send in my name.'

Thought for today
Yesterday we said that Jesus is in heaven. We've also said that Jesus is with us. How can Jesus be with us and in heaven? It's because of the Holy Spirit who comes to us. He is sweet, gentle, loving and truthful. And he links us with Jesus.

To talk about
Even vicars don't fully understand about the Holy Spirit. What other things do you find hard to understand?

A prayer to say
Father God, thank you for the Holy Spirit. Amen.

September 1

God's fans

Bible reading: Psalm 34 verses 1, 2 and 4
'I will praise the Lord at all times ... The poor will hear and be glad ... I asked the Lord for help and he saved me from all that I feared.'

Thought for today
When we love God, and when he answers our prayers, we want to praise him. That means we want to talk (or sing) about how good, and great and loving God is. Poor people, that is, people who know they need God's help, feel hopeful and glad when they hear us praising God.

To talk about
Why did the man who wrote today's verse praise God?

A prayer to say
Father God, I praise and thank you for all your love and kindness. Amen.

SEPTEMBER 2

A secret weapon

Bible reading: Psalm 8 verse 2

'You have taught children and babies to sing praises to you. And so you silence your enemies.'

Thought for today

Kim was in bed feeling ill. To cheer herself up, she started to sing songs about Jesus. And after a while, she didn't feel so ill! Today's verse says that when children praise God, then God's enemies grow quiet.

To talk about

Who does God specially teach to sing?

A prayer to sing

'*Praise him, praise him, All ye little children. God is love. God is love. Amen.*'

The angels' song

Bible reading: Psalm 89 verses 15 and 16
'Happy are the people who know how to praise you ... They praise your goodness.'

Thought for today
What does today's verse say about the people who know how to praise God? All the angels in heaven are praising God. Today's prayer is from the angels' song to Jesus. As you say it, you are joining in with the angels.

To talk about
Do you know a praise song you can sing or say?

A prayer to say
'The Lamb [Jesus] who was killed is worthy to receive power, wealth, wisdom and strength, glory, honour and praise.' Amen.

250

SEPTEMBER 4

The song of the universe

Bible reading: Psalm 148 verses 1 and 7
'Praise the Lord from the heavens. Praise the Lord from the earth.'

Thought for today
Trees and flowers, birds with song,
Mountains high and rivers long,
Sun and moon, stars and sky,
Praise you, Father, in heaven so high.
    May all the earth its praises bring
      To love the Lord, our heavenly King.

To talk about
Suggest a way of finishing this sentence: 'Praise
God because ...'

A prayer to say
Praise the Lord! Amen.

SEPTEMBER 5

Days of praise

Bible reading: Acts 2 verses 46 and 47
'The believers ... broke bread in their homes, happy to share their food with joyful hearts. They praised God, and all the people liked them.'

Thought for today
Today's verses are about the very first Christians. They were so happy that Jesus had died and come to life again, that they couldn't stop talking about him. They would go to each others' houses, and share their food with gladness and love for each other, praising God all the time.

To talk about
Why do you think that all the people liked the very first Christians?

A prayer to say
Thank you, Father God, that I can share what I have. Amen.

Ways of praise

Bible reading: Psalm 149 verse 3

'They should praise him with dancing. They should praise him with tambourines and harps.'

Thought for today

Anything that makes people say, 'Isn't God great!' counts as praise. So we can praise God in lots of ways: not only by what we say or sing, but by what we do. Today's verse describes two ways of praising God.

To talk about

Can you think of any other ways of praising God without words?

A prayer to say

Dear Father God, help me to bring praise to you, not only by what I say and sing but by everything I do. Amen.

Sunday songs

Bible reading: Psalm 100 verses 2, 4 and 5

'Come before him with singing ... Come into his courtyards with songs of praise ... The Lord is good.'

Thought for today

The man who wrote Psalm 100 wanted God's people to go singing into the Temple (church) in Jerusalem to worship God. When we go to church to praise God with other Christians, we are showing everyone that we trust God and love him.

To talk about

Something you like about going to church.

A prayer to say

Father God, I want all the people who live around me to know that you are a good and loving and great God. Amen.

Prison praise

Bible reading: Acts 16 verse 30
The jailer said, 'Men, what must I do to be saved?'

Thought for today
Paul and Silas had been thrown into prison. But instead of grumbling they were singing praises to God. Suddenly there was an earthquake. The doors opened, and their chains fell off. But they didn't run away. When the jailer saw all this, he wanted to become a Christian, too.

A prayer to sing
'Come let us sing: Praise to our King,
Jesus our King, Jesus our King:
This is our song, who to Jesus belong:
Glory to Jesus, to Jesus our King.'
(By S C Horne)

To talk about
What do you think Paul said to the jailer?

SEPTEMBER 9

Bad times

Bible reading: Habakkuk 3 verses 18 and 19
'But I will still be glad in the Lord. The Lord God gives me my strength ... He leads me safely.'

Thought for today
Sometimes everything seems to go wrong. We sing praises to God. But nothing gets better. Habakkuk thought about that. Suppose there is disaster all around. Suppose there is no food to eat. What then? He will still praise God. And God will make him strong and show him what to do.

To talk about
Bad times you've known or heard about.

A prayer to say
Dear heavenly Father, thank you because you are with me in the bad times. Amen.

September 10

The king's song

Bible reading: Psalm 96 verses 1 and 2
'Sing to the Lord a new song ... Sing to the Lord and praise his name.'

Thought for today
King David wrote Psalm 96. Here are some more words from the psalm. 'Every day tell how he saves us. The Lord made the skies. Tell the nations, "The Lord is king." Let the skies rejoice and the earth be glad.'

To talk about

'A new song' (in today's verse) probably meant 'a new tune'. Can you make up a tune to go with these words (or alter the words to fit a tune)?

A prayer to say
Father God, I praise you because you are King over all the people in the world. Amen.

September 11

Sing a silent song

Bible reading: Ephesians 5 verse 19
'Sing and make music in your hearts to the Lord.'

Thought for today
When you're waiting in a queue, or wandering down the street, or doing nothing in particular, what can you do? You could sing, but if you sing aloud, people might stare, or tell you to stop making that dreadful noise. But you can sing to Jesus in your heart (that means, in your mind and with your feelings).

To talk about
Good or bad things about hanging around in queues.

A prayer to say
Thank you, Father, that you hear my songs even if I can't sing out loud. Amen.

September 12

Hannah's thank you song

Bible reading: 1 Samuel 2 verse 1
Hannah sang, 'The Lord has filled my heart with joy ... I am glad because you have helped me.'

Thought for today
Hannah was very sad. 'Lord God,' she cried, 'please may I have a baby.' In those days, every boy helped his father and learned his father's job. But Hannah promised that if she could have a baby boy he would train to work full-time for God.

To talk about
A time when God has helped you.

A prayer to say
Thank you for giving Hannah a baby boy. And thank you because her baby, Samuel, grew up to love and obey you. Amen.

Up a tree

Bible reading: Luke 19 verse 4

'[Zacchaeus] ran ahead to a place where he knew Jesus would come.'

Thought for today

'Let me through, I can't see a thing!' The little fat man jumped and pushed. But nobody moved. He looked round and saw a tree with big branches. Zacchaeus hitched up his clothes and hauled himself up. Now he would have a good view of Jesus as he walked by.

To talk about

What are some good and bad things about being small?

A prayer to say

Dear Lord Jesus, Zacchaeus wanted to find out about you and didn't give up. Help me to be like that. Amen.

I spy up a tree

Bible reading: Luke 19 verse 2

'Zacchaeus was a wealthy, very important tax-collector [working for the country's enemies].'

Thought for today

'So that's who Jesus is!' thought Zacchaeus, peering down through the leaves. Jesus was walking right under the tree, talking to the people around him.

Suddenly Jesus stopped. He was looking up. He said, 'Zacchaeus, hurry and come down! I must stay at your house today.'

To talk about

How do you think Zacchaeus felt?

A prayer to say

Dear Lord Jesus, thank you because nothing is hidden from you. Amen.

SEPTEMBER 15

Crashing down

Bible reading: Luke 19 verse 6
'Zacchaeus came down quickly.'

Thought for today
Zacchaeus was beaming as he walked through the streets with Jesus. But all the people were angry. 'Look at the kind of man Jesus stays with! A liar and a cheat and a thief.'

To talk about
Why were the people angry?

A prayer to say
Dear Lord Jesus, thank you because you love everybody, even the people everybody else hates. Amen.

SEPTEMBER 16
A turn-around

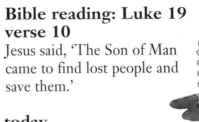

Bible reading: Luke 19 verse 10
Jesus said, 'The Son of Man came to find lost people and save them.'

Thought for today
Zacchaeus was thrilled because Jesus was now his friend. How could he say thank you? This is what he did. He said to Jesus, 'I will give half my money to the poor. And if I've cheated anyone, I'll pay that person back four times more!'

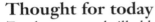

To talk about
What do we mean when we say, 'Actions speak louder than words'?

A prayer to say
Dear Lord Jesus, thank you for loving me, and helping me. Amen.

SEPTEMBER 17

Bonkers for conkers

Bible reading:
Psalm 136 verse 1

'Give thanks to the Lord because he is good. His love continues for ever.'

Thought for today

Sarah had spent the morning collecting conkers. She picked out a bright, shiny conker and gave it to Rick. He grabbed it and raced off without saying anything.

To talk about

Something to thank God for.

A prayer to say

Heavenly Father, help me not to be like Rick. Help me always to say thank you to you. Amen.

SEPTEMBER 18

Inside out

Bible reading: Luke 21 verse 1
'Jesus saw some rich people putting their gifts into the Temple money box.'

Thought for today
The rich people put lots of money into the money box. But then a poor widow came and gave two small coins. Jesus said, 'The widow gave more than all those rich people. They kept plenty of money for themselves. But she gave all she had.'

To talk about
Do you remember what God said when he chose David to be King? (Look back to July 22.)

A prayer to say
Dear Lord Jesus,
thank you because
you see our inside
feelings and reasons.
Amen.

September 19

Glad to give

Bible reading: 2 Corinthians 8 verses 11 and 12

Paul wrote, 'Give from what you have ... Your gift will be judged by what you have, not by what you do not have.'

Thought for today

Sarah had just a little pocket money. She spent some on sweets, and some she put into the box at church. In his letter to a group of Christians Paul said, 'Be glad to help poorer people. If you have a lot of money, give a lot, but if not, give what you can.'

To talk about

Ask your mum or dad who they give money to.

A prayer to say

Dear Lord Jesus, thank you for all you have given me. Amen.

September 20

Sshhhhh!

Bible reading: Matthew 6 verses 3 and 4
Jesus said, 'When you give to the poor, give very secretly ... Your Father can see what is done in secret, and he will reward you.'

Thought for today
There are two ways of giving for God. One is to tell everybody and boast about what we are doing. The other is to give without people outside our family knowing, and without showing off.

To talk about
Which way of giving does Jesus say is better?

A prayer to say
Dear Father God, when I do anything good, help me not to show off about it. Amen.

SEPTEMBER 21

Plenty of everything

Bible reading: 2 Corinthians 9 verse 8
'And God can give you more blessings than
you need. Then you will always have plenty of
everything. You will have enough to give to every
good work.'

Thought for today
We need never be afraid of giving too much, for our heavenly Father
always cares for us. If our aim is to help other grown-ups and children,
God will make sure we have all we need.

To talk about
Can you finish this sentence: 'God gives us plenty of everything so that ...'

A prayer to say
'I am trusting you,
Lord Jesus,
 Never let me fall;
I am trusting you for ever,
And for all.' Amen.
(By Frances R Havergal)

September 22

A harvest song

Bible reading: Psalm 65 from verses 10 to 13

'You cause rain to fall on the ploughed fields ... You give the year a good harvest ... The hills are covered with happiness. The pastures are full of sheep. The valleys are covered with grain. Everything shouts and sings for joy.'

Thought for today

Once a year, at harvest or thanksgiving, we especially remember that we depend on God to send the sun and rain to make our food grow. And we thank him.

To talk about

What would you like about living on (or going for a holiday to) a farm?

A prayer to say

'All good gifts around us
Are sent from heaven above.
Then thank the Lord,
O thank the Lord,
For all his love.'
(By M Claudius)

SEPTEMBER 23

A wedding

Bible reading: John 2 verse 1
'There was a wedding in the town of Cana in Galilee.'

Thought for today
The bride and groom were dressed in beautiful rich clothes and wore lots of jewellery. They were like a king and queen. The guests put on their best clothes and gave presents. Jesus' mother was there, and so were Jesus and his friends.

To talk about
Ask your mum and dad what they like to remember about their wedding.

A prayer to say
Weddings are so exciting. Thank you for weddings. Amen.

270

SEPTEMBER 24

Disaster!

Bible reading: John 2 verse 3
'Jesus' mother said to him, "They have no more wine."'

Thought for today
The wedding feast often lasted for a week and much of that time was spent eating and drinking. It was very important to have plenty of food and drink. But at the wedding in Cana something terrible happened - before the party was over, they ran out of wine.

To talk about
Have you ever been to a party when something has gone wrong?

A prayer to say
Dear Lord Jesus, help me always to come to you for help, just as Mary did. Amen.

SEPTEMBER 25

The right time

Bible reading: John 2 verse 4
'Jesus said, "Dear woman, why come to me? My time has not yet come."'

Thought for today
In those days there was no tea or coffee. People drank water or wine. At the Cana wedding, only the servants and Mary and now Jesus knew there was no wine. Jesus said to Mary that it was not the right time for everyone to know who he was.

To talk about
Getting the timing right is important - even in small things like cooking or gardening. Can you think of any examples?

A prayer to say
Dear heavenly Father, thank you because you know the right time for everything. Amen.

September 26

Gallons of water

Bible reading: John 2 verse 5
'His mother said to the servants, "Do whatever he tells you to do."'

Thought for today
Jesus pointed to six big stone water jars. 'Fill the jars with water,' he said. The servants filled them to the top (it came to 960 pints). 'Now take out some water and give it to the head-waiter' (who was organising the wedding).

To talk about
What do you think the servants said to each other?

A prayer to say
The servants did what you told them to. Help me to obey you, Jesus. Amen.

273

SEPTEMBER 27

Cheers!

Bible reading: John 2 verse 8
'So the servants took the water to the master.'

Thought for today
The head-waiter tasted the water. He was astonished. 'What delicious wine!' he said.

To talk about
What's one of the best parties you've been to? What made it good?

A prayer to say
Dear Lord Jesus, thank you for changing the water into wine, so that the wedding party was not ruined. Amen.

September 28

Finish with a flourish

Bible reading: John 2 verse 11
'So in Cana of Galilee, Jesus did his first miracle.'

Thought for today
The head-waiter spoke to the bridegroom. He said, 'People always serve the best wine first. But you have saved the best wine until now.' He had no idea where the good wine had come from. But the servants knew.

To talk about
In Jesus' time people mostly drank wine mixed with water. What do you prefer to drink?

A prayer to say
*Dear Lord Jesus,
thank you because you
do everything
perfectly. Amen.*

SEPTEMBER 29

The best

Bible reading:
John 2 verse 11
'Jesus showed his glory and his followers believed in him.'

Thought for today
In this miracle Jesus was teaching us many things about himself and about why he had come. He showed us how much our heavenly Father loves us. When Jesus changed the water into wine it was very good wine. Our Father God loves to give us what's best for us.

To talk about
What does today's verse say happened as a result of the miracle?

A prayer to say
Thank you, heavenly Father, for all your good gifts to us, and most of all for sending Jesus. Amen.

SEPTEMBER 30

A new way

Bible reading: John 10 verse 10
'I came to give life - life in all its fullness.'

Thought for today

The religion of the Jews had many rules. The water pots were an example. They were for special washing that had to be done as part of the religion. But when Jesus changed plain water into sparkling wine he was showing that he was changing the old religion.

To talk about
Something you like about this Bible story.

A prayer to say

Dear Father God, thank you because Jesus has showed us a sparkling new way of pleasing you - a way of love and trust in him. Amen.

A present

Bible reading: Ephesians 6 verse 1

'Children, obey your parents the way the Lord wants. This is the right thing to do.'

Thought for today

Did you know that you are a present from God to your mum and dad? He gave you to them and they care for you. Every day they teach you, and every day there is something to learn. You can help them by doing what they say.

To talk about

What are the children learning to do in today's pictures?

A prayer to say

Dear Father God, thank you for my mum and dad. Help me to obey them. Amen.

OCTOBER 2

Growing up

Bible reading: Luke 2 verses 51 and 52

'Jesus went with them [Mary and Joseph] to Nazareth and obeyed them ... Jesus continued to learn more and more and to grow physically. People liked him and he pleased God.'

Thought for today

'Jesus, will you fetch the broom?'
'Jesus, keep an eye on your sister.'
'Yes, you can go out now.'
Jesus didn't say, 'I'm the Son of God, I don't have to do what you say.' He obeyed Mary and Joseph.

To talk about

Jesus learnt his father's job. Do you remember what that was? (See March 6)

A prayer to say

Dear Jesus, help me to be loving and kind to my parents, as you were to Mary and Joseph. Amen.

October 3

Two ears

Bible reading: Proverbs 1 verse 8
'My child, listen to your father's teaching.'

Thought for today
When you are very busy, playing with your toys or looking at a book, or watching a good programme on the television, it's difficult to pay attention to your daddy. But he may be saying something important.

To talk about
When your dad starts speaking to you - what should you do?

A prayer to say
Heavenly Father, help me to listen to my mum and dad with both ears. Amen.

OCTOBER 4

Watch out!

Bible reading: Proverbs 1 verse 8
'And do not forget your mother's advice.'

Thought for today
Don't run out on the road ... Don't touch the electric socket ... Don't play with knives ... Sometimes it seems that mummies spend their time making up rules. But if you keep the rules you will be kept safe.

To talk about
Is there anything you keep doing wrong because you keep forgetting?

A prayer to say
Heavenly Father, help me to pay attention and remember. Amen.

OCTOBER 5

Happy families

Bible reading:
Proverbs 23
verses 22, 24 and 25
'Listen to your father, who
gave you life, and do not forget
your mother when she is old ... The
father of a good child is very happy. Make
your father and mother happy. Give your mother a reason to be glad.'

Thought for today
Think of all your mum and dad do for you, like working to earn money,
washing, ironing, sewing ... And when you're naughty they still love you,
even when they tell you off. Give them a kiss, and tell them you love them!

To talk about
Can you think of some more things your mum
and dad do for you?

A prayer to say
Father God, help
me to show my
mum and dad
that I love them.
Amen.

OCTOBER 6

Who's in charge?

Bible reading: 1 Peter 5 verse 5
'Younger men should be willing to be under older men.'

Thought for today
At church you usually like the leaders, teachers and helpers. But sometimes they seem old and boring. But God chose them, and gave them their jobs in the church. Today's verse tells younger people to respect older leaders, and listen to them.

To talk about
In your church, which leaders and helpers do you especially like?

A prayer to say
Dear Father God, help me not to show off and act big in church. Amen.

283

OCTOBER 7

The Jesus way

Bible reading: John 15 verses 10 and 12

Jesus said, 'I have obeyed my Father's commands, and I remain in his love. In the same way, if you obey my commands, you will remain in my love ... This is my command: love each other as I have loved you.'

Thought for today

Jesus said these words on the night before he died. They sum up some of the important things he wanted to say. Jesus loved his heavenly Father so much that he always obeyed him. What did Jesus command? Listen to today's verse again.

To talk about

What does loving people mean? (January 11 and April 18 give some pointers.)

A prayer to say

Father, I want to obey you and be like Jesus. Amen.

OCTOBER 8

Coming alongside

Bible reading: 2 Peter 1 verse 7
'... and to your service for God, add kindness for your brothers and sisters in Christ.'

Thought for today
In your Sunday club at church, a girl is crying. You say, 'What's the matter?' She says she's lost her collection. What can you do? Some children are making fun of an old lady in the church. You tell your mum and dad and you all talk to her.

To talk about
Can you think of some other ways of being kind?

A prayer to say
Dear Lord Jesus, I want to be like you. Help me to be kind. Amen.

A friend called Ruth

Bible reading: Ruth 1 verse 8

Naomi said, 'You have been very kind to me and to my sons who are now dead.'

Thought for today

Old Naomi's husband and sons had died. So she was leaving the country of Moab and going back alone to her own country. She said goodbye to Ruth, her daughter-in-law who came from Moab. But Ruth said, 'I'm going with you.' Ruth went with Naomi and cared for her mother-in-law.

To talk about

Ruth was brave and kind. Do you know anyone like Ruth?

A prayer to say

Heavenly Father, thank you for Ruth's kindness to Naomi. Amen.

OCTOBER 10

Shipwreck!

Bible reading: Acts 28 verses 1 and 2
'When we [Luke and Paul] were safe on land, we learned that the island was called Malta ... the people who lived there... welcomed all of us.'

Thought for today
'Shipwreck!' All the ship's crew and passengers came swimming to the beach or were washed up, clinging to pieces of wood. It was raining and very cold but the people on the island made a big fire and brought food.

To talk about
Do you remember reading about this storm? Who helped Paul?
(See February 22)

A prayer to say
Father God, thank you for the kind people of Malta.
Amen.

287

OCTOBER 11

Shirts and coats

**Bible reading:
Acts 9 verses 36
and 37**
'There was a follower [of Jesus]
named Tabitha ... She was always
doing good and helping the poor
... Tabitha became sick and died.'

Thought for today
'Hurry, please come with us,' the men said to
Peter. They took him to an upstairs room. There he
saw some very poor women, who were crying. 'Look at
the shirts and coats Tabitha made for us.' Peter knelt and
prayed and Jesus brought Tabitha back to life.

To talk about
In what ways was Tabitha kind?

A prayer to say
*Dear Jesus, thank you for your
loving kindness in bringing
Tabitha back to life. Amen.*

OCTOBER 12

The end of the world

Bible reading: Matthew 25 verse 34
'Then the King will say to the good people on his right, "Come. My Father has given you his blessing. Come and receive the kingdom God has prepared for you" ...'

Thought for today
Jesus said today's words. The scene is the end of the world, and Jesus is on his throne. He is welcoming the good people into heaven. He goes on to say, 'I was hungry, and you gave me food. I was thirsty, and you gave me something to drink ...' (Continued tomorrow)

A prayer to say
Lord Jesus, thank you for the kind things that these good people did. Amen.

To talk about
Do you know of any organisations who help hungry people?

OCTOBER 13

A surprise

Bible reading: Matthew 25 verse 35

'I was alone and away from home, and you invited me into your house. I was without clothes, and you gave me something to wear. I was sick, and you cared for me. I was in prison, and you visited me.'

Thought for today

When Jesus said these things to the good people, they were very surprised. 'Lord,' they said, 'when did we do all this?' And Jesus said, 'Anything you did for any of my people you also did for me.'

To talk about

What are the people doing in today's picture?

A prayer to say

Lord Jesus, I'm little, I can't do all these things. But when I have the chance, please help me to do what I can, and not turn away. Amen.

OCTOBER 14   Our friends the animals

Bible reading: Proverbs 12 verse 10
'A good man takes care of his animals.'

Thought for today
When God made the world, he put Adam and Eve in charge of the animals. People must be kind to the animals, birds and fish in our world. They must not treat them in unkind ways.

To talk about
In what ways can you be kind to pets, birds or other animals?

A prayer to say
Please help all the people who are working to protect and care for animals, fish and birds. Amen.

OCTOBER 15

A wicked queen

Bible reading: 1 Kings 18 verse 4
'At one time Jezebel was killing all the Lord's
prophets [a prophet was God's messenger].'

Thought for today
Hundreds of years before Jesus was born, a wicked
king and queen ruled over Israel. Queen Jezebel
wanted to stop the people trusting God. She said,
'You must all
worship my god,
Baal, because only
Baal will give you rain for your crops.'

To talk about
Do you know any lies that people say about
God today?

A prayer to say
*Heavenly Father, help me never to
believe people who speak against you.
Amen.*

OCTOBER 16

Dare to be different

Bible reading: 1 Kings 17 verse 1
'Elijah said to King Ahab, "I serve the Lord, the God of Israel ... I tell you the truth. No rain or dew will fall during the next few years unless I command it."'

Thought for today
'Rubbish!' said Elijah to King Ahab. 'My God made the world, and the rain falls when he says.' Then, before Ahab and Jezebel could throw him into prison, Elijah went away.

To talk about
What can you do if you see something wrong happening at school?

A prayer to say
Lord God, thank you for Elijah's courage in speaking up for you. Amen.

OCTOBER 17

Ravens for waiters

Bible reading: 1 Kings 17 verse 3
The Lord said to Elijah, 'Leave this place. Go east and hide near Kerith Ravine.'

Thought for today
For week after week, there was no rain. While the grass withered and the crops died, King Ahab hunted for Elijah. In hiding by a little brook, Elijah had water to drink, and every morning and evening the birds brought him bread and meat.

To talk about
Do you remember reading about Elijah earlier this year?
Who brought him food? (Check it out: February 28.)

A prayer to say
Heavenly Father, thank you for keeping Elijah safe, and for sending him food. Amen.

OCTOBER 18

Into enemy country

Bible reading: 1 Kings 17 verse 7
'After a while the brook dried up because there was no rain.'

Thought for today
God said to Elijah, 'Go to the town of Zarephath. I have told a widow to take care of you.' Zarephath was in the country of Sidon. Its king was Jezebel's father. Its god was Baal. At the town gate Elijah saw a widow collecting wood to make a fire.

To talk about
Why didn't Elijah say, 'Not Zarephath! It's too dangerous!'

A prayer to say
Lord God, thank you for choosing somebody unimportant, just a poor widow, to look after Elijah. Amen.

295

OCTOBER 19

Don't worry

Bible reading: 1 Kings 17 verses 10 and 11
Elijah asked the widow, 'Would you bring me a little water in a cup? ... Please bring me a piece of bread, too.'

Thought for today
The widow had only a handful of flour and a little oil - enough to make one last meal for herself and her son. 'Don't worry,' Elijah said. 'Bake a loaf for me and then cook for yourself. As long as the dry weather lasts there will be flour in your jar and oil in your jug.'

To talk about
Can you remember reading about another widow who Jesus saw? What did she do? (Look back to September 18.)

A prayer to say
Father God, thank you because nothing is impossible for you, and you look after your people. Amen.

OCTOBER 20

A promise

Bible reading: 1 Kings 18 verse 1
'During the third year without rain, the Lord spoke his word to Elijah ...
"Go and meet King Ahab."'

Thought for today
Elijah met Ahab's servant Obadiah. 'Tell Ahab that I am here.' 'I daren't,'
Obadiah said. 'You'll vanish again and Ahab will kill me.' Elijah said, 'I
serve the Lord of heaven's armies. As surely as the
Lord lives, I will stand before Ahab today.'

To talk about
Have you ever been let down by someone
who said they'd do something and didn't?

A prayer to say
*Lord God, help me
always to remember
how great and
powerful you are.
Amen.*

OCTOBER 21

The showdown

Bible reading: 1 Kings 18 verse 18
Elijah said to Ahab, 'You have not obeyed the Lord's commands. You have followed Baal.'

Thought for today
It was time for a showdown. Elijah said, 'Tell the country's leaders to meet me at Mount Carmel, and bring the 450 prophets of Baal and the 400 prophets of Asherah (another pretend god).' At Mount Carmel, Elijah stood in front of the people.

To talk about
What sort of person was Elijah?

A prayer to say
Heavenly Father, please help all people today who stand up for you. Amen.

OCTOBER 22

Time to choose

Bible reading: 1 Kings 18 verse 21

Elijah said, 'How long will you try to serve both Baal and the Lord? If the Lord is the true God, follow him. But if Baal is the true God, follow him.'

Thought for today

Elijah spoke to all the leaders of his people. 'Make up your minds,' he said. 'Serving two gods gets you nowhere. It's time to choose.' All the people looked at him. And said nothing.

To talk about

Why do you think the people said nothing?

A prayer to say

Lord God, help me not to half obey and half trust you. Amen.

OCTOBER 23

The test

Bible reading: 1 Kings 18 verse 24
'All the people agreed that this was a good idea.'

Thought for today
Elijah told the prophets of Baal to build a pile of stones (an altar) and put wood and meat on the top. 'I'll do the same,' he said. 'Then you ask Baal to send fire to burn your meat and I'll ask my God. The God who sends fire is the true God.'

To talk about
How did Elijah already know that God answers prayer?

A prayer to say
Father God, in Elijah's time the situation was desperate. True faith was almost dead. Thank you because today we have Jesus with us. Amen.

OCTOBER 24

Prophets-go-round

Bible reading: 1 Kings 18 verse 25
'Then Elijah said to the prophets of Baal, "There are many of you. So you go first."'

Thought for today
The 450 prophets of Baal pranced and danced, hopped and skipped, round the altar. From morning to evening they shouted, 'O Baal, answer us. O Baal, answer us.' Elijah laughed. 'Call louder. Maybe he's busy or on a journey.' No fire came.

To talk about
The Baal prophets were phoney. Do you know of any sham mumbo-jumbo today?

A prayer to say
Lord God, thank you because you are the only God who answers prayer. Amen.

OCTOBER 25

Fire from heaven

Bible reading: 1 Kings 18 verse 30
'Elijah rebuilt the altar of the Lord because it had been torn down.'

Thought for today
Elijah prayed, 'Lord, answer my prayer. Show these people that you, Lord, are God. Then the people will know that you are bringing them back to you.' Then fire came down from heaven. It burnt up the meat, the wood, and the stones. The people fell down and cried, 'The Lord is God.'

A prayer to say
'My whole being praise the Lord. Flames of fire are your servants.'
(From Psalm 104)

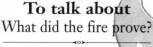

To talk about
What did the fire prove?

OCTOBER 26

Rain!

Bible reading: 1 Kings 18 verse 42
'Elijah climbed to the top of Mount Carmel
[facing the sea].'

Thought for today
Elijah knelt and prayed. Seven times he sent his servant
to stare out over the sea. The seventh time the servant
said, 'I see a small cloud.' Soon the sky was covered in
dark clouds and heavy rain began to fall. That was the
end of the famine.

A prayer to say
*Thank you, Lord God, because
you didn't give up on the people.
You wanted them to trust you
again. Amen.*

To talk about
What do you like about this story
about Elijah?

Top dog and underdog   OCTOBER 27

Bible reading: 1 Corinthians 12 verses 7 and 8
Paul wrote, 'Something from the Spirit can be seen in each person, to help everyone. The Spirit gives one person the ability to speak with wisdom ...'

Thought for today
Christians meet with other Christians to worship God and learn about him. And God's Spirit gives one person the skill to preach, another to teach, or cook or manage money - there are many ways of helping. In the church at Corinth some Christians were saying, 'But I'm more important.'
(Continued tomorrow)

To talk about
What job might you like to do in the church when you're grown up?

A prayer to say
Please help Christians not to boast about what they can do. Amen.

OCTOBER 28

A helping hand

Bible reading: 1 Corinthians 12 verse 25
Paul wrote to the Christians in Corinth, 'God wanted the different parts to care the same for each other.'

Thought for today
Paul wrote, 'Your body has many different parts, and all the parts are important. Your eyes can't say to your hands, "I don't need you." Your head can't say to your feet, "I don't need you."' It's the same with Christians. When we belong to God's family, we all need each other.

To talk about
What abilities and ways of helping do people in your family have?

A prayer to say
Lord God, thank you for teaching us that in your family we are all equally important. Amen.

OCTOBER 29

Toothache?

Bible reading: 1 Corinthians 12 verse 26
Paul wrote, 'If one part of the body suffers, than all the other parts suffer with it. Or if one part of our body is honoured, then all the other parts share its honour.'

Thought for today
If your tooth hurts, then all your body is upset. And in God's family it should be the same. We should share in each other's worries and sadness and happiness. Paul wrote, 'Be happy with those who are happy. Be sad with those who are sad.'

To talk about
Do you remember a time when Jesus cried?
(Look back to August 24.)

A prayer to say
Thank you, heavenly Father, for friends who understand how I feel. Amen.

Hands up

Bible reading: Hebrews 3 verse 13

'But encourage each other every day.'

Thought for today

'Put your hands up if you've prayed to God today,' said Wesley's teacher. Wesley looked round. Nobody's hand was up. Very slowly he put up his hand. Then four other children put up their hands.

To talk about

How else can we encourage each other?

A prayer to say

Keep me shining, Lord,
Keep me shining, Lord,
In all I say and do.
That the world may see
Christ lives in me
And learn to love him too.

(by K B Wilkinson)

OCTOBER 31

To sum up

Bible reading:
Galatians 5
verse 14

'The whole law is made
complete in this one
command: "Love your
neighbour as you love
yourself."'

Thought for today
When you want to do
something to hurt someone,
like kicking or punching or
making fun, think: would you like those things to happen to you? No!
That's part of what it means to love someone as you love yourself. Treat
other children as you'd like them to treat you.

To talk about
How do you like children to treat you?

A prayer to say
*Father God, help me as I try to keep
this law. Amen.*

November 1

Keeping time

Bible reading: Ecclesiastes 3 verses 1 and 2
'There is a right time for everything ... There is a time to plant and a time to pull up plants.'

Thought for today
Black storm clouds, thunder, lightning, winter snow and freezing showers, soft, warm sunshine, flowers appearing. Bees are buzzing, bright sun shining. Leaves are falling, dark is coming. Life is turning, growing in me, stretching out and on. All the seasons have a meaning, teaching me of God.

To talk about
Your favourite things in the year.
Fill in the gaps in the prayer.

A prayer to say
Dear Father God, thank you for spring: for lambs and ...; thank you for summer; for ...; for autumn; for conkers and ...; for winter and ... Amen.

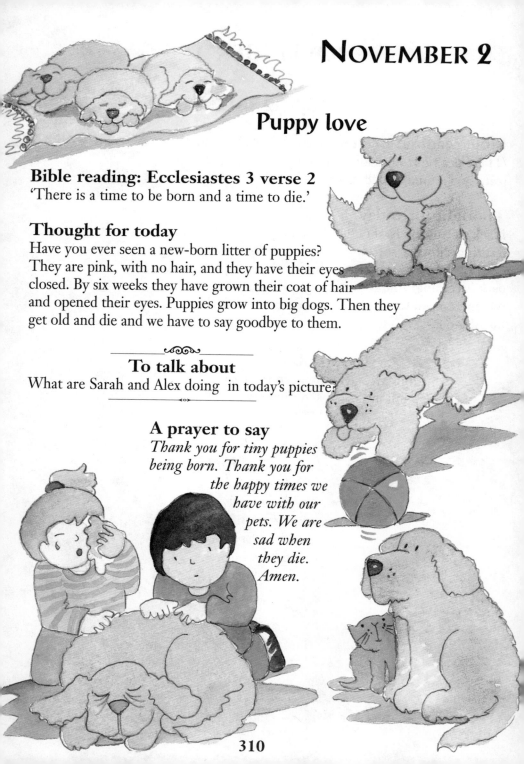

Puppy love

Bible reading: Ecclesiastes 3 verse 2
'There is a time to be born and a time to die.'

Thought for today
Have you ever seen a new-born litter of puppies?
They are pink, with no hair, and they have their eyes
closed. By six weeks they have grown their coat of hair
and opened their eyes. Puppies grow into big dogs. Then they
get old and die and we have to say goodbye to them.

To talk about
What are Sarah and Alex doing in today's picture?

A prayer to say
*Thank you for tiny puppies
being born. Thank you for
the happy times we
have with our
pets. We are
sad when
they die.
Amen.*

November 3

Alive with Jesus

Bible reading: 1 Thessalonians 4 verses 13 and 14

'We want you to know about those who have died. We do not want you to be sad as others who have no hope. We believe that Jesus died and that he rose again. So, because of Jesus, God will bring together with Jesus those who have died.'

Thought for today

When people we love die, we're sad because we miss them. But we are not sad for them - they will be with Jesus. And one day we'll see them again. To find out more, look back to March 28.

To talk about

Do you remember the two meanings of the word 'heaven'?
(Look back to March 28.)

A prayer to say
Thank you, Jesus, because when we die we'll see you, and live with you. Amen.

NOVEMBER 4

Tears and smiles

**Bible reading:
Ecclesiastes 3 verse 4**
'There is a time to cry and a time
to laugh. There is a time to be sad
and a time to dance.'

Thought for today
When we feel sad, it helps to
cry. Jesus cried when his
friend Lazarus died. When we feel happy it's great to jump and leap and
skip and twirl round and round.

To talk about
A time when you were feeling happy. What did you do?

A prayer to say
*Thank you Lord Jesus for tears when
I'm sad, and for dancing and singing
when I'm happy. Amen.*

NOVEMBER 5

Jigsaws and puzzles

Bible reading: Romans 8 verse 28
'We know that in everything God works for the good of those who love him.'

Thought for today
Jo's mum was very ill. Dave's dad lost his job. Sometimes things happen that are hard to understand. We say, 'Why did God let this happen?' It's a puzzle. We don't know. But we do know God loves us and helps us. One day we will understand.

To talk about
What are the children doing in today's picture?
What does a piece of jigsaw have to do with today's thought?

A prayer to say
Dear Lord Jesus,
please bring good
out of the bad
things that happen.
Amen.

November 6

Love that's for real

Bible reading: Hebrews 12 verses 6 and 9
'The Lord corrects those he loves ... We have all had fathers here on earth who punished us. And we respected our fathers.'

Thought for today
In school, a teacher told off a naughty boy. And so the boy tore up all the pages in his book! The other children said, 'His mum spoils him.' Your mum loves you. That's why she won't let you get away with naughty things.

To talk about
Look at today's picture. What is Alex holding? What should his mum do?

A prayer to say
Dear heavenly Father,
thank you because my
mummy loves me and that's
why she tells me off when
I'm naughty. Amen.

Stand up for Jesus!

Bible reading: Matthew 5 verse 11

Jesus said, 'People will say bad things about you and hurt you ... because you follow me. But when they do these things to you, you are happy.'

Thought for today

When you are good, and want to be like Jesus, sometimes some other children don't like you. When you won't join in with them, and when you say 'no' to wrong things, sometimes they may call you names. People got angry with Jesus, too.

To talk about

Has this ever happened to you or to someone you know?

A prayer to say

Thank you, Jesus, that you help me to be brave and happy for you. Amen.

PRIVATE

November 8

Love that's for always

Bible reading: Romans 8 verse 38
'Yes, I am sure that nothing can separate us from the love that God has for us.'

Thought for today
Paul wrote today's words. He also said this prayer: 'I pray that you can understand how wide and how long and how high and how deep Christ's love is. Christ's love is greater than any person can ever know. But I pray that you will be able to know that love.'

To talk about
Sarah is waving goodbye to her dad.
What is she saying to him?

A prayer to say
Dear Lord Jesus, please help me and my mum and dad and … to be happy because you love us so much. Amen.

November 9

A comforting thought

Bible reading: 2 Corinthians 1 verses 3 and 4
'And he is the God of all comfort. He comforts us every time we have trouble ...'

Thought for today
Sometimes we feel sad, or lonely or afraid or ill. Sometimes people laugh at us or say unkind things. Sometimes no one seems to understands how we feel. But God knows and he comforts us in many ways. The January 24 thought for today tells us one way God comforts us.

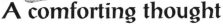

To talk about
Who or what do you find comforting?

A prayer to say
Dear Father God, thank you that you are the God of all comfort, and you always understand how I feel. Amen.

NOVEMBER 10

A shady place

Bible reading: Psalm 91 verse 1
'Those who go to God Most High for safety will be protected by God All-Powerful.'

Thought for today
God comforts us by his promises in the Bible. Today's verse is one promise. In Africa the sun is burning hot. But if you sit under a shady tree, the tree will protect you from sunburn. When we pray to God for help, he protects us from harm.

To talk about
What do you like doing on or by trees?

A prayer to say
Thank you, heavenly Father, for trees with wide branches where we can sit and be cool on a hot day. Thank you for keeping us safe like a big tree. Amen.

A welcome for you

Bible reading: John 6 verse 37

'The Father gives me my people. Every one of them will come to me, and I will always accept them.'

Thought for today

The poor, blind beggar sat by the road as Jesus passed by, and called, 'Please help me.' 'Be quiet,' everyone said. 'The teacher has no time for the likes of you.' But the beggar yelled out, 'Jesus!' And Jesus stopped, spoke to him, and healed him.

To talk about

The story of blind Bartimaeus is in Mark 10 verses 46 to 52.
Why do you think Jesus healed him?

A prayer to say

Thank you, Lord Jesus, for today's comforting verse. You never turn away anyone who calls to you. Amen.

November 12

Tidings of comfort and joy

Bible reading: Hebrews 4 verse 15
'For ... [Jesus] is able to understand our weaknesses. When he lived on earth, he was tempted in every way that we are, but he did not sin.'

Thought for today
Jesus learnt to be a carpenter. I expect he sometimes banged his hand or cut himself. He had friends who were sometimes unkind to him. He knows what it's like to be very sad, and to be very happy. We can talk to him about everything and he understands.

To talk about
If Jesus walked into your room now,
is there anything you would like to ask him?

A prayer to say
Thank you, Lord Jesus, that you understand how I feel. Amen.

NOVEMBER 13

Whistle a happy tune

Bible reading: Acts 16 verse 25
'About midnight Paul and Silas were praying and singing songs to God.'

Thought for today
Beaten up by the crowd. Thrown into the darkest, coldest, dampest part of
the prison. Their feet fastened to large blocks of wood. Cold and in pain.
Just for preaching about Jesus. What did Paul and Silas do in prison?
Listen to today's verse again.

To talk about
Do you remember how today's story ends?
Look back to September 8.

A prayer to say
*Dear Lord Jesus, please help me to sing
and trust you when I have problems.
Amen.*

Down in the dumps?

Bible reading:
Philippians 2
verse 25

'Epaphroditus is my brother in Christ ... When I needed help, you sent him to me.'

Thought for today

Paul wrote today's words from prison. He had badly needed help, and his friends had sent Epaphroditus to see him. Down in the dumps? A friend makes us laugh. Got a problem? A friend listens. Over and over again, God comforts us as our family and friends comfort us.

To talk about

Who is a comforting friend in today's picture?

A prayer to say

Thank you, Father God, for my family and friends who help me. Amen.

November 15

Trouble shooters

Bible reading: Galatians 6 verse 2
'Help each other with your troubles.'

Thought for today
This is a true story from Africa. 'Quick! Hide in the forest,' said the older girl. The children ran and hid while the the soldiers burnt down their village huts. Then the children ran on and on until at last they came to a safe place where people wanted to look after them.

To talk about
Do you know anyone with any problems who you can help in any way?

A prayer to say
Dear Father God, thank you for keeping those children safe. Thank you for the people who gave them love and shelter and looked after them. Amen.

NOVEMBER 16
Friends

Bible reading: 1 Thessalonians 4 verses 17 and 18

'And we will be with the Lord for ever. So comfort each other with these words.'

Thought for today

There's a little girl in Mozambique in Africa whose parents were killed in the war. Now she lives in an orphanage. Sometimes she cries at night for her mummy and daddy. Then the other children comfort her, and they pray for each other.

Sentence

To talk about

Listen again to today's verse. What could you say to comfort the little girl whose parents had died?

A prayer to say

Thank you, Father God, for your comfort. Thank you because we can comfort one another. Amen.

November 17

All the love you need

Bible reading: Isaiah 66 verse 13

God said, 'I will comfort you as a mother comforts her child.'

Thought for today

You may not have a mother or father. But God has all the love you need to comfort you. Ask him for his help, and like the orphan children we read about yesterday, God will find a way to comfort you.

To talk about

Do you remember some of the ways God comforts us?

A prayer to say

Dear Father God, thank you because you comfort me like a mother.

November 18

Bad dreams

Bible reading: 2 Corinthians 1 verse 4

'He comforts us every time we have trouble, so that we can comfort others when they have trouble. We can comfort them with the same comfort that God gives us.'

Thought for today

'Don't! Help!' Alex screamed. The scream woke him up. He was terrified. He made himself sing some songs about Jesus. Slowly he felt better and fell asleep again. Next day Kim said she was scared at night. So Alex told her about how Jesus had helped him.

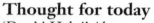

To talk about

A good or bad dream you've had.

A prayer to say

Dear Lord Jesus, thank you for the comfort you give me. When I have the chance, help me to pass this on to other people. Amen.

NOVEMBER 19

A scary job

Bible reading: Joshua 1 verse 9

'Be strong and brave ... don't be afraid. The Lord your God will be with you wherever you go.'

Thought for today

Moses, God's great leader, was dead. Who would take over as commander of the people? God chose Joshua. Joshua had to lead God's people back home into their own country. They had to fight ferocious enemies. Could Joshua do it? Today's verse gives God's promise to Joshua.

To talk about

Do you know any leaders (in school, church, or your town)?

A prayer to say

Dear Father God, please help all leaders in our world and churches today. Please help them to be good and brave and trust you. Amen.

November 20

Problem 1: a river

Bible reading: Joshua 3 verse 15

'During harvest time the [river] Jordan is flooded. So the river was at its fullest.'

Thought for today

Joshua and his desert fighters were ready to march into their land. But there was a massive problem: a wide, deep river to cross, and no bridge. 'Tell those in front to cross the river,' said God to Joshua. The first men stepped right into the raging water - and then - God stopped the water flowing.

To talk about

God worked a miracle for Joshua. Do you remember who else God worked a miracle like this for? (Check it out: July 20.)

A prayer to say

Thank you, Lord God, because everyone walked across the dried-up river. Thank you for being with Joshua, just as you had promised. Amen.

November 21

Problem 2: a city

Bible reading: Joshua 5 verses 13 and 14

'Joshua was near Jericho. He looked up and saw a man standing in front of him ... The man [said], 'I have come as the commander of the Lord's army.'

Thought for today

Joshua's army had walked across the river bed. But now, blocking the way into the country, was Jericho, a great, strong city with high walls. What could Joshua do? He walked towards the city, by himself. And there in front of him, he saw a stranger, with a sword. It was an angel!

To talk about

What do you think Joshua was doing when he was out walking by himself?

A prayer to say

Dear Father God, thank you for sending your angel to Joshua. Amen.

NOVEMBER 22

Trumpets for weapons

Bible reading: Joshua 6 verse 2
'Then the Lord spoke to Joshua. He said, "Look, I have given you Jericho, its king and all its fighting men."'

Thought for today
The angel told Joshua God's battle plan. It seemed crazy! He said, 'March around the city with your army once every day. Do this for six days. On the seventh day march round the city seven times while the priests blow their horns and all the people shout.'

To talk about
Trumpets were used in battle to scare the enemy.
Do you know the battle music used by the Scots?

A prayer to say
Dear Father God, help me, like Joshua, to pray and ask you when I don't know what to do. You have the best plans. Amen.

November 23

Tumbling down

Bible reading: Joshua 6 verse 7
'Then Joshua ordered the people, "Now go! March around the city."'

Thought for today
On the seventh day, as the priests blew their trumpets and the people shouted, there was a creaking and cracking, a shivering and shaking, a ripping and roaring, and down fell the walls of Jericho with a crash and a cloud of dust.

To talk about
Can you think of any times when you've prayed to God and he's helped you?

A prayer to say
Dear Father God, help me also to trust you and obey you. Amen.

Last words

Bible reading: Joshua 23 verses 10 and 11
'The Lord your God fights for you, as he promised to do. So you must be careful to love the Lord your God.'

Thought for today
Joshua is now very old. He calls the leaders together for his very last speech. It's a victory speech. But it's also a warning. 'Watch out!' says Joshua. 'Be brave and strong. God will keep you safe. But you must do your part. You must obey God.'

To talk about
Who is reading today's thought with you?
Ask what their last words would be.

A prayer to say
Dear Father God, help all the people in our churches today to remember Joshua's last words. Amen.

NOVEMBER 25

No messing about

Bible reading: Psalm 147 verse 11
'The Lord is pleased with those who fear him, with those who trust his love.'

Thought for today
God made the universe. All the power in the universe belongs to him. Millions of angels do what he says. So we should feel fear, and awe and wonder as we pray to him. We can't mess about with God.

To talk about
Is there someone you look up to, someone you like so much that you feel ashamed to let them know you've done something wrong?

A prayer to say
Dear Father God, you are so great. Help me to feel wonder and awe as I pray to you. I can hardly believe it makes you happy when I trust you. Amen.

November 26

Simply amazing

Bible reading: Psalm 139 verses 13 and 14
'You made my whole being. You formed me in my mother's body. I praise you because you made me in an amazing and wonderful way.'

Thought for today
There is nobody in the world like you. Everyone and everything is different, and amazing, and God made all of it. So he doesn't have a problem understanding things or people.

To talk about
There are amazing things about the world and our bodies. What do you think is amazing?

A prayer to say
Thank you, heavenly Father, because you understand everything and know everything. Amen.

NOVEMBER 27

First aid

**Bible reading:
Psalm 91 verse 15**
'They will call to me and
I will answer them. I will
be with them in trouble.'

Thought for today
When Kim cut her knee,
she cried. Her knee went
on hurting
for a long time, but her
Mummy read her stories to help her forget. Our Father God knows all
about things like cut knees, and will send us just the help we need when we
need it.

To talk about
Have any of your friends hurt themselves when you were with them?
What did you do?

A prayer to say
*Thank you, Father God, for my mummy,
and all the people who help me when I'm sad
or hurt. Amen.*

NOVEMBER 28

First things first

Bible reading: Mark 1 verse 35

'Early the next morning, Jesus woke and left the house while it was still dark. He went to a place to be alone and pray.'

Thought for today

Jesus was busy. Hundreds of people wanted his help. Did he say, 'I'm too busy to pray. God will understand'? No. Jesus made time to pray to his Father God. He needed God to guide and help him.

To talk about

Why do you think people say 'hands together and eyes closed' when you pray?

A prayer to say

Dear Father God, help me always to remember that I need you. Help me always to make time to pray. Help me always to remember to pray. Amen.

Prayer power

Bible reading: Luke 6 verses 12 and 13

'Jesus went off to a mountain to pray ... The next morning, Jesus called his followers to him. He chose 12 of them.'

Thought for today

Jesus had a decision to make. He wanted to choose 12 helpers and it was important to choose the right people. So what did he do first of all? Listen to today's verse again.

To talk about

Jesus prayed early in the morning and at night. Do you have a best time for praying?

A prayer to say

Dear Lord Jesus, every time I have to make a choice, help me to remember to pray for your help. Amen.

NOVEMBER 30

In the orchard

Bible reading: Hebrews 5 verse 7

'While Jesus lived on earth, he prayed to God and asked God for help. He prayed with loud cries and tears ... And his prayer was heard because he left it all up to God.'

Thought for today

At the end of his life, Jesus knew that one of his best friends had deserted him. He knew he would be captured and killed. So he went to an orchard in the hills and prayed. And he said to God, 'Do what you want, not what I want.'

To talk about

Jesus prayed for God's will to be done. Can you remember another time when he said these words? (Clue: a well known prayer.)

A prayer to say

Dear Father God, whenever I feel sad or afraid help me always to talk to you about it. Amen.

The coming of the King

Bible reading: Mark 13 verse 26

'Then people will see the Son of Man [Jesus] coming in clouds with great power and glory.'

Thought for today

Advent is the name that Christians give to the weeks in December before Christmas. The word 'Advent' means 'coming'. In Advent we get ready for the coming of Jesus at Christmas. We also think about the time when Jesus will come again. At his Second Coming, everyone will see Jesus, the King.

To talk about

Do you have an Advent calendar? What sort do you like best?

A prayer to say

Lord Jesus, thank you because one day you will come to our world again, and everyone will see that you are a great king. Amen.

DECEMBER 2

Hurrah for that Day

Bible reading: Mark 13 verse 27
'The Son of Man [Jesus] will send his angels all around the earth. They will gather his chosen people from every part of the earth.'

Thought for today
When Jesus comes again you and your family, and everyone who trusts him, will go together to be with him in his kingdom. You won't be split up. Everyone will be happy. It will be like a wedding party. Wrong things will be put right when Jesus comes again.

To talk about
What wrong things in the world would you like to see disappear?

A prayer to say
(A prayer prayed by the first Christians)
Lord Jesus,
please come quickly,
Amen.

DECEMBER 3

A six million dollar question

Bible reading: Mark 13 verse 4
Jesus' friends said, 'Tell us, when will all
these things happen?'

Thought for today
'When will you come again?' That's what Jesus' friends
wanted to know. And this is what Jesus said: 'No one knows
when that day or time will be. The Son and the angels don't know. Only
the Father knows. Be careful. Always be ready. You don't know when that
time will be.'

To talk about
What do you think will be exciting about Jesus' Second Coming?

A prayer to say
*Lord Jesus, your Second Coming will
be wonderful and exciting. Help me
never to forget that you are coming
again. Amen.*

December 4

Red alert

Bible reading: Mark 13 verse 37

Jesus said, 'I tell you this, and I say this to everyone: "Be ready!"'

Thought for today

Jesus said, 'The owner of a big house went on a trip to a far away country. Before going, he gave his servants jobs to do. And he said, "I could be back at any time. So make sure you don't slack. Do your work well. Be on the look-out."'

To talk about

In this story, the owner of the house is Jesus. Who do you think the servants are?

A prayer to say

'Living, you loved me, Dying, you saved me. Rising, you justified, freely for ever. One day you're coming - O glorious day!' Amen
(From a hymn by J W Chapman)

DECEMBER 5

Everything you need

Bible reading: 2 Timothy 3 verse 17

'Using the Scriptures, the person who serves God will ... have everything he needs to do every good work.'

Thought for today

Would you like to be the best you can be for God? Then start with the little things you can do for him. How can we know what pleases God? Today's verse tells us how to find out.

To talk about

What little things can you do?

A prayer to say

Dear Lord Jesus, I like to think of you by my side each day. Please help me to do the little things that please you. Amen.

DECEMBER 6

Love alert

Bible reading:
Ephesians 5 verse 2
'Live a life of love. Love other people just as Christ loved us.'

Thought for today
When we love somebody we never want to harm them, but keep them near us, please them, protect them and just be with them. Our heavenly Father wants us to live with his love in our hearts. That is the best way to be ready for Christmas and Jesus' Second Coming.

To talk about
What are some of the things your mum and dad have to do to get ready for Christmas?

A prayer to say
Thank you for all my family and friends who I love. Amen.

December 7

Looking out and looking up

Bible reading: 1 Timothy 2 verse 2
'You should pray for kings and for all who have authority [who are in charge of other people].

Thought for today
We talk to people we love. Prayer is talking to our Father God because we love him. And praying is another way of being ready - and helping others to be ready - for Jesus' coming. Who does today's verse tell us to pray for?

To talk about
Do you know any other leaders or important people who you can pray for?

A prayer to say
Father, I ask you to care for and guide ... Please make them loving and wise, and brave to stand up for you. Amen.

345

December 8

Prayer warriors

Bible reading: 1 Timothy 2 verse 2

'Pray for the leaders so that we can have quiet and peaceful lives - lives full of worship and respect for God.'

Thought for today

Governments use soldiers to keep peace in countries. But it is love that brings real peace. We can be soldiers of love and pray that God will bring peace in countries where there is war.

To talk about

Do you know of any countries where there is war?

A prayer to say

Thank you, Father, for your peace. Please bring your love and peace to countries where there is war. Amen.

THE WORLD

DECEMBER 9

Friends-in-prayer

Bible reading:
Ephesians 1 verse 17
Paul wrote, 'I always pray to the
God of our Lord Jesus Christ ...
I pray that he will give you a
spirit that will make you wise in
the knowledge of God.'

Thought for today
Paul wrote and told his friends that he prayed for them all the time. He
wanted them to know Jesus, his wonderful friend. We can pray for our
friends, too. We can pray that they will know Jesus more and more each
day.

To talk about
Do you have a friend who specially needs your prayers today?

A prayer to say
Father, I pray that my friends, and
my family and I may all see you
more clearly, follow you more
nearly and love you more dearly,
day by day. Amen.
(Based on a prayer by Frances
Chichester).

347

December 10

Count me out!

Bible reading: Jonah 1 verses 1 and 2

'The Lord spoke his word to Jonah son of Amittai, "Get up, go to the great city of Nineveh and preach against it. I see the evil things they do."'

Thought for today

Jonah was shocked. Preach to the people of Nineveh? Certainly not. They were the enemy. If he preached to them, they might pray. And God might forgive them. Preach in Nineveh? Not likely! Death to Nineveh! Jonah packed his bags and set off - in the opposite direction.

To talk about

Do you know any naughty children? What do they do?

A prayer to say

Please, Father God, help us to listen to you and obey you. Amen.

Nineveh

Where's the spinach?

Bible reading: Jonah 1 verse 3

Jonah 'found a ship that was going to the city of Tarshish [in Spain]. Jonah paid for the trip and went aboard. Jonah wanted ... to run away from the Lord.'

Thought for today

The ship set sail. Then God sent a strong wind. The wind was howling and waves were washing over the boat. It was in danger of breaking up and the sailors were terrified. Where was Jonah? He was fast asleep.

To talk about

Have you ever been on a big or little boat? What did you like about it?

A prayer to say

Father God, you loved the people of Nineveh. Help us to care for other people. Amen.

Man overboard!

Bible reading: Jonah 1 verse 6
'The captain of the ship came and said, "Why are you sleeping? Get up! Pray to your God ... Perhaps he will save us!"'

Thought for today
'I'm running away from God,' Jonah said to the sailors. 'Throw me into the sea and the wind will stop.' 'We can't do that!' But the storm got worse. The sailors cried to God, 'Please don't let us die because we're killing Jonah.' Then they threw him into the sea.

⏤⏤⏤⏤⏤

To talk about
Jonah was still cross. He didn't want to pray.
What makes you cross?

A prayer to say
Heavenly Father, when I feel cross, help me to talk to you about how I feel. Amen.

Yum! Yum! What's in my tum?

Bible reading: Jonah 1 verse15
'Then the men picked up Jonah and threw him into the sea. So the sea became calm.'

Thought for today
Jonah sank deeper and deeper into the sea. Weeds wrapped around his head. He landed on the bottom of the ocean. And at last he cried out to God to save him. Then God sent a big fish to Jonah. Along it swam and swallowed him down whole.

To talk about
What do you think Jonah said when he was in the fish?

A prayer to say
Thank you, Father God, for saving Jonah. Amen.

351

DECEMBER 14

Underwater transport

Bible reading: Jonah 2 verse 6
'I thought I was locked in this prison for ever. But you saved me from death.'

Thought for today
Jonah was inside the fish for three days and three nights. Then God spoke to the fish. It swam to the shore and spat Jonah out of its stomach. Up Jonah came, on to the dry land.

To talk about
What do you think made Jonah feel happy when he was lying on the beach?

A prayer to say
'Lord, I prayed to you and you heard my prayers. Lord, I will praise and thank you.' Amen.
(Part of Jonah's prayer while he was in the fish.)

DECEMBER 15

No kidding

Bible reading: Jonah 3 verses 1 and 2
'Then the Lord spoke his word to Jonah again. The Lord said, "Get up. Go to the great city of Nineveh."'

Thought for today
This time Jonah obeyed God. Nineveh was a large and beautiful city with parks and palaces, libraries and temples. But its people were wicked. Jonah walked into the city centre and started to preach: 'In forty days God will destroy you.' (So he hoped!)

⌘⌘⌘

To talk about
It was brave of Jonah to preach in Nineveh. Do you know anybody who you think is brave?

A prayer to say
Father God, thank you because Jonah got up and went to Nineveh and gave them your message. Amen.

All change

Bible reading: Jonah 3 verse 5
The people of Nineveh believed in God ... They put on rough cloth to show how sad they were.'

Thought for today
The king of Nineveh put on rough, scratchy cloth. He wouldn't sit on his royal throne. He sat down in ashes. He told everybody: 'Wear this rough cloth. Your animals, too. Stop eating and drinking. And stop doing wrong things.' All the people kept telling God how sorry they were. And God forgave them.

To talk about
What do you think Jonah thought when God forgave the people?

A prayer to say
Heavenly Father, thank you because the people listened to Jonah and were sorry. Amen.

DECEMBER 17

Jonah the moaner

Bible reading: Jonah 3 verse 10
'God saw what the people did. He saw that they had stopped doing evil things. So ... he did not punish them.'

Thought for today
Jonah was angry. 'I knew this would happen,' he shouted at God. 'It's why I didn't want to come. I knew you'd go and forgive them. That's just what you're like. You're kind.' 'I wish I was dead,' Jonah said to God. 'Please kill me!'

To talk about
Why was Jonah so fed up?

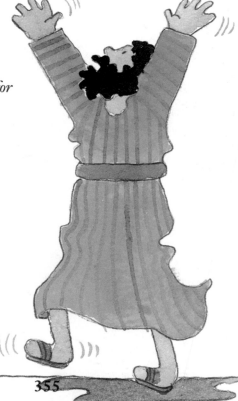

A prayer to say
Heavenly Father, thank you for being loving and kind, and ready to forgive. Amen.

DECEMBER 18

Seeing red

Bible reading: Jonah 4 verse 5
'Jonah went out and sat down east of the city ...
He was waiting to see what would happen to
the city.'

Thought for today
God made a tall plant grow up. Its big leaves
sheltered Jonah from the sun. But the next day
the plant withered and died. The sun blazed
down on Jonah's head. He felt ill and he was
angry because the plant had died. 'I wish I was
dead!' he said.

To talk about
Jonah was sorry for himself, and for the
plant. Who wasn't he sorry for?

A prayer to say
*Heavenly Father, thank you
because you are in charge of
everything that happens.
Amen.*

DECEMBER 19

Lessons in love

Bible reading: Jonah 4 verse 9
'But God said this to Jonah, "Do you think it is right for you to be angry because of the plant?"'

Thought for the day
'Yes!' said Jonah. 'And I'll stay angry till I die!' Then God said, 'You took pity on a plant? Well what about the great city of Nineveh, with more than 120,000 people, who don't know what they are doing, and all the animals? Surely I can be sorry for them?

To talk about
What are some of the things we learn about God from the story of Jonah?

A prayer to say
Heavenly Father, thank you for your loving care for all people, and animals, too. Amen.

December 20

Something amazing

Bible reading: Luke 1 verse 27
'[Mary] was engaged to marry a man named Joseph.'

Thought for today
Do you know someone who's going to get married? It's very exciting. Mary lived in the hillside village of Nazareth. She was going to marry Joseph. While she was planning and preparing for her wedding, something amazing happened - an angel came to visit her!

To talk about
Do you remember what the word 'angel' means? (Look back to February 22.)

A prayer to say
Heavenly Father, thank you for weddings, and for angels. Amen.

A message for Mary

Bible reading: Luke 1 verse 38
'Mary said, "I am the servant girl of the Lord. Let this happen to me as you say!"'

Thought for today
The angel's name was Gabriel, and he had a message from God. God was going to give Mary a wonderful gift - a baby boy. Mary was to call him Jesus. He would be God's Son, but God wanted Mary to have him and care for him till he was a man.

To talk about
Listen to today's verse again - from this, what can you learn about Mary?

A prayer to say
Heavenly Father,
thank you for the gift
of Jesus to Mary. Amen.

DECEMBER 22

A dream

Bible reading: Matthew 1 verse 19
'Mary's husband, Joseph, was a good man.'

Thought for today
An angel spoke to Joseph in a dream. 'Don't be afraid to marry Mary,' the angel said. 'She will have a baby son, born by the power of the Holy Spirit. You must call him Jesus.' Joseph went to see Mary, and they were married straightaway.

To talk about
Do you remember what the name 'Jesus' means? (Look back to February 11.)

A prayer to say
Dear Father God, thank you for Joseph's love for Mary and his trust in you. Amen.

A king's town

Bible reading: Luke 2 verse 1

'At that time, Augustus Caesar [the Roman Emperor] sent an order to all people in the countries that were under Roman rule. The order said that they must list their names in a register.'

Thought for today

Everyone had to go back to the town their families came from. Mary and Joseph had to travel to Bethlehem, 90 miles away. This was the town King David had been born in, hundreds of years earlier. Joseph was descended from King David. It was tiring for Mary, travelling all that way on a donkey.

To talk about

Mary was looking forward to the birth of her baby.
What are you looking forward to this Christmas?

A prayer to say

*Heavenly Father, thank you for keeping
Mary safe as she travelled. Amen.*

DECEMBER 24

No room!

Bible reading: Luke 2 verse 7
'There were no rooms left in the inn.'

Thought for today
At Bethlehem, the inn was full. But there was space in the stable. This was probably a cave, behind or below the inn. Here travellers' donkeys were tethered. There was straw, and shelter from the wind, and peace from the crowds. But imagine sleeping in a stable!

To talk about
If this were to happen today, and the hotels were full, where might a modern Mary and Joseph go?

A prayer to say
Father God, please help all people who are cold and tired and have no home. Thank you for my warm home.
Amen.

A King in a stable

Bible reading: Luke 2 verse 6
'While Mary and Joseph were in Bethlehem, the time came for her to have the baby.'

Thought for today
Mary wrapped baby Jesus in long strips of cloth, as mothers did in those days, and she laid him in a manger. This was the box where hay was put for the animals to eat.

To talk about
Giving and receiving presents is one way of being happy at Christmas. What presents do you especially like?

A prayer to say
'O come, let us adore him, Christ the Lord.' Amen.

DECEMBER 26

Songs in the night

Bible reading: Luke 2 verse 8
'That night, some shepherds were in the fields nearby watching their sheep.'

Thought for today
Perhaps the shepherds were sitting round the fire, talking about the day. Suddenly there was a great brightness all around and an angel appeared. The angel said, 'Don't be afraid,' and told them about the wonderful baby king, born in Bethlehem. Then there were lots more angels, all singing praises to God.

To talk about
What happy things have happened in your family this Christmas?

A prayer to say
Thank you, Father God, for Jesus. Amen.

It's true!

Bible reading: Luke 2 verse 20

'Then the shepherds went back to their sheep, praising God and thanking him for everything that they had seen and heard. It was just as the angel had told them.'

Thought for today

The angels disappeared, and the light faded. All was quiet in the hills. 'What are we waiting for? Come on!' The shepherds raced down to Bethlehem. And it was true! There he was, lying in the manger, just as the angel had said. The Saviour, Christ the Lord.

To talk about

Do you have a favourite carol you can sing?

A prayer to say

God's own Son. How wonderful! Thank you, Father God. Amen.

Palace plots

Bible reading: Matthew 2 verse 2
The wise men asked, 'Where is the baby who was born to be the king of
the Jews? ... We have come to worship him.'

Thought for today
Away to the east there lived some wise men. They saw a new star, and
knew that a king had been born. They travelled to the palace in Jerusalem.
What a shock for King Herod! 'Try Bethlehem,' he murmured. 'And when
you've found the new king, come and tell me so I may worship him, too.'

To talk about
What do you think cruel King Herod may have been thinking?

A prayer to say
Heavenly Father, thank you for sending the Christmas star. Amen.

DECEMBER 29

Kingly gifts

Bible reading: Matthew 2 verse 9
'The wise men heard the king and then left.
They saw the same star they had seen in the east.
It went before them until it stopped above the
place where the child was.'

Thought for today
When the wise men saw the star again they were extremely happy. Mary,
Joseph and Jesus were now in a house. The wise men went in, bowed down
to their King, and gave Jesus rich presents: gold, frankincense and myrrh
(two expensive, sweet-smelling liquids).

To talk about
The Bible doesn't say how many wise men
there were. Why do you think we say there
were three?

A prayer to say
*Lord Jesus, we worship
you, too. Amen.*